DIMENSIONS OF RURAL POVERTY

DIMENSIONS OF RURAL POVERTY

Dr. G. ERRAIAH, M.A., M.Phil., Ph.D.,
Associate Professor
Department of Economics
Sri Venkateswara University
Tirupati - 517 502 (A.P.), INDIA

SERIALS PUBLICATIONS
New Delhi (India)

First Published-2005

ISBN : 81-86771-76-X

Published by

Head Office : **SERIALS PUBLICATIONS**
4, B.S.S. Hall, Khyber Pass Market
Civil Lines, Delhi-110054 (India)
Phone : 23245225
Fax : 91-11-23272135
E-mail: serials@satyam.net.in

Branch Office : 4830/24, Prahlad Street, Ansari Road
Darya Ganj, New Delhi-110002 (India)

Printed at : R.K. Offeset Process, Naveen Shahdara

PREFACE

Poverty alleviation in India is an age old ambition. In 19th Century Dadabai Naoroji, distinguished economist felt that India is rich in economic resources and culture but Indians are poor because of foreign rule. Hence independence is achieved and to alleviate poverty in short span India opted planned macro level approach with the assumption that fruits of development should percolate among all sections and regions of the people.

But the noted research study "Poverty in India" conducted in 1971 by V.M Dandekar and N. Rath based on NSS data disclosed the fact that Trickle Down Theory did not work properly, as a result rich become richer and poor become poorer in the first two decades of independence. This study also brings forth various poverty dimensions namely - poverty in India is rural in nature since urban poverty is the over flow of rural poverty and the incidence of poverty is the highest (57%) among agricultural labours.

In the light of the study after 1970's Micro level approach is followed to assist the poor directly. In this process Govt. of India initiated the worlds largest Dairy Development Program i.e., Operation Flood Program in three phases with the assistance of EEC and World Food Pragramme. The earlier evaluation studies expressed confronted views about this programme benefits reach to rural poor. In this context in this book an attempt has been made to study the impact of operation flood program on agricultural labours in Andhra Pradesh.

This book is a slightly modified version of the doctoral thesis, I have submitted to the Srivenkateswara University, Tirupati, India and which earned me the degree of Doctor of Philosophy (Economics) in 1995.

I take this opportunity to express my heart-felt thanks to all those who have helped me directly or indirectly in completion of this book.

I am highly indebted to my research supervisor Prof.L.Kannainah Naidu, Dept of Econometrics, S.V.University for his constant interest, encouragement and valuable guidance. I thank all the faculty members of Economics for their timely assistance.

With pleasure I put on record my gratitude to Dr. P Purushotham Naidu, Dr. M.Mohan and Sri Venkatadri, Faculty members, National Institute of Rural Development and Sri Sudhakar Reddy, Center for Economic and Social Studies, Hyderabad for their valuable suggestions.

I indebted to Chittoor Cooperative Milk Union Officials - Sri G. Yerram Naidu, General Manager, Sri E.Lakshmanna, Regional Assistant Dairy Engineer, Sri. K. Jeevarathnam Naidu, Sri S. Raghavaiah and especially sample milk co-operative member households and others for providing me the necessary information.

I am thankful to the librarians of Institute for Social and Economic Change, Bangalore, National Institute of Rural Development, Hyderabad, S.V.University Tirupati, for placing at my disposal the necessary books and records.

I express my deep sense of gratitude to my teacher Prof. B. Raghavulu Naidu, Dr.V.Balakrishnam Naidu and Late Dr. K. Suresh Babu co-research scholars for their valuable assistance at all levels.

I put on record my feeling of appreciation for my wife Shireesha for her continuous encouragement. My appreciation is highly due to my children G.Maneesha and G.Himaja for the delightful company whenever I required.

Finally, I once again thank all my friends who have helped either directly or indirectly to complete the work.

CONTENTS

1

STATEMENT OF THE PROBLEM AND METHODOLOGY

No Society can surely be flourishing and happy of which, by far the greater part of the members are poor and miserable.

—*Adam Smith, 1776*

1.1 Statement of the Problem

Food is one of the basic needs of life. Since beginning of time, man's activities and very existence have been governed by quest for food. Only relatively recently developed countries have been able to provide adequate food supplies for their population. Many less developed countries still suffer from frequent famines caused by drought and other natural disasters.

Historically systematic writing and research about poverty is largely a post-war phenomenon. Earlier, the explanation for the existence of poverty was sought interms of individual deficiencies of character and productive skills. Hence, no attempt was made to formulate a deliberate economic development strategy for alleviation of poverty and raising living standards.

It is after Keynesian revolution the consensus has changed. Poverty phenomenon is viewed in terms of social origin and causation, rather than individual inhibitions and inadequacies.

Recently world recognised the fact that poverty any where is dangerous to prosperity every where and the focus of national and international efforts are directed to increase the productivity of poor.

The main objective of the present governments in the world is to maximise the social welfare. The removal of poverty is the first step in this direction. In India since independence macro level approach was followed till early seventies by expecting that over all country's growth which itself leads to alleviate poverty. But research studies conducted by individuals, agencies and governments at different levels revealed that the fruits of development did not percolate to the poor; instead the living conditions of the poor were further deteriorated.

Around 1970 there was a shift in the development policy of the third world countries including India, from growth orientation to growth with equity orientation. It was realised that it was not enough for development planning to pursue a high rate of growth; it is important that the growth is accompanied by improved distribution, employment and reduction in poverty. This shift in development concern from growth to growth with equality in 1970's was reflected in rural development policy in India. Beginning with Small Farmers Development Agency Programme, accompanied by host of other programmes for the weaker sections and backward regions of the country, the concern for growth with equality reached its culmination in extending the poverty alleviation programmes to entire country in the year 1980. It is claimed that every third rupee spent in our planning now is spent on poverty alleviation alone.

Irrespective of all these planned efforts to reduce poverty, Indian poor accounted one-third of the world poor in 1990 and India is classified as one of the worst poverty stricken nations of the world. Hence, there is need to understand the nature and dimensions of poverty in India further.

A critical examination of the national development efforts revealed that five categories of rural workers viz., marginal farmers, small farmers, agricultural labourers, non-agricultural labourers and rural artisans who constitute the development scenario of rural India have not been benefitted from the developmental efforts.

Among all these categories, agricultural labourers constitute a large section of population in India. They are also a less articulate section of the workers, mainly due to lack of organization and low level of education. Agricultural labourers drawn form socially and economically backward classes constitute the poorest section of the rural poor in India.

India occupies first place in possession of bovine population and second place in milk production in the world. Dairy subsector being a fast growing one, best suits the arable lands, provides productive employment and income to the under employed rural poor and helps to meet the consumer needs in urban centres.

In India dairy proved mostly a small man enterprise and has wide scope for its promotion. In view of all these merits Government of India has been implementing Operation Flood Programme since 1970 in three phases upto 1994 so as to achieve sustainable cooperative dairy sector with the assistance from European Economic Community and World Food Programme.

Chittoor district is a part of the four districts of Rayalaseema region in Andhra Pradesh which is noted for famines in South India. Agricultural labourers accounted for 35 per cent of total work force which is much higher than national average (25 per cent) and frequent occurrences of drought compels the labour force to migrate from rural to urban sector.

In 1981-82 the Bureau of Economics and Statistics, Government of Andhra Pradesh, conducted a sample socio-economic survey for the first time with a view to have a bench mark macro-level data on the socio-economic conditions of the rural population and to identify the target groups for various rural development programmes in the State. As per this study, Chittoor district ranks as the poorest district in the state with 61.25 per cent of families below poverty line.

In the district organised dairy was initiated in 1969 by the Government of Andhra Pradesh and further milk shed was included as part of Operation Flood-II in 1981. There after dairy emerged as the prominent income generating activity with those of Drought Prone Area Progamme/Integrated Rural Development Programme. The district obtained the credit as the best district in the state for implementing crossbreed programme and the district claimed 40 per cent of crossbreed cows of Andhra Pradesh. Hence, Chittoor Milk Union (Dairy Union) one among the top ranking milk unions in Andhra Pradesh. According to National Dairy Development Board Appraisal Report 1990, Chittoor milk union procured about 24 per cent of the milk procured in Andhra Pradesh.

Chittoor district is not an exception to regional variations. It can be divided into three natural divisions, namely Eastern region with plains, Central region with mid land areas and Western region with upland/hilly areas. Dairying in all these regions is not uniformly prosperous.

Since dairying is more prosperous in the district on one hand and on the other because of high proportion of agricultural labourers as well as their high incidence of poverty, in addition to regional variations with in the district, an attempt is made to study the impact of dairy development through Operation Flood programme on agricultural labourer house holds in three regions of the district in Andhra Pradesh.

1.2 Objectives

The following are the major objectives of the study.

1. To study the nature and dimensions of rural poverty in India.
2. To study the dairy development and its impact on rural poor in India.
3. To analyse the dairy milk procurement in three regions of Chittoor district.
4. To assess the role of diary development through Operation Flood Programme in generation of income and employment among agricultural laborur households.

5. To evaluate the impact of dairy development through Operation Flood Programme in eradication of poverty among agricultural labourers.

1.3 Hypotheses

The following hypotheses will be examined.

1. Eradication of rural poverty in India is a matter of effective implementation of redistributive measures.
2. Dairy development in India through Operation Flood Programme has many beneficial effects on rural poor.
3. There is significant increase in dairy milk procurement in three regions of Chittoor district.
4. Dairy development through Operation Flood Programme has generated additional income and employment in agricultural labour households.
5. Dairy development through Operation Flood Programme has significant impact on poverty of agricultural labourers.

1.4 Methodology

To examine the hypotheses related to the study both secondary and primary data are used.

The secondary data on different aspects of the problem are drawn form International publications like World Bank, World Food Organisation, ILO. Relevant data are also collected from the records of Government of India, Reserve Bank of India, National Dairy Development Board, Government of Andhra Pradesh and from other sources of research publications. Further, necessary information is also collected form Chittoor District Official and non-official records.

1.5 Sampling Procedure

On the basis of agro-climatic conditions, Chittoor district has been divided into three natural divisions namely, western, central and eastern regions to reduce the heterogeneity in sample households.

In Chittoor district there are 889 milk cooperatives as on December 1992. For this study, 20 milk cooperatives are chosen randomly in proportion to the total cooperatives in each region. From each selected society, the list of agricultural labour households is obtained of which 10 per cent of the households have been selected using random procedure. To evaluate the impact of operation flood programme on economic conditions of agricultural labour households, 10 per cent of the agricultural labour households who are not members of the milk cooperative society in the respective villages are also covered in this study and these households constitute the control group.

On the whole, the study covers 98 agricultural labour households who are members of the milk cooperative societies and 128 non-member households. The distribution of the sample households is presented in the following table:

Table 1
Region-wise and Category-wise Distribution of Sample Agricultural Labour Households.

S. No	*Region*	*No.of sample milk cooperatives*	*Member households*	*Non-member households*	*Total*
1.	Central	13	76	28	104
2.	Eastern	3	12	50	62
3.	Western	4	10	50	60
	Total	20	98	128	226

The primary data from the selected households are obtained by personal interview method for the reference year 1992-93. Primary data on various socio-economic aspects of milk producers in Chittoor district are collected using well designed schedules. To analyse data relevant statistical tools are used.

1.6 Chapter Scheme

First chapter contains the statement of the problem, objective of the study, hypotheses proposed to be examined and methodology.

Second chapter explains the concept of poverty, extent of global poverty, nature of rural poverty, characteristics of the rural poor, Indian poverty in the world perspective, review of literature on Indian poverty, incidence of poverty among agricultural labour households, public policy and the rural poor in India and degree of success of redistrubutive measures in eradication of rural poverty in India.

Chapter three covers, the importance of dairy in India, Plans, Policies and programmes of Government of India in the development of cattle and dairy; Operation Flood project, its objectives and achievements; implementing agencies of Operation Flood and the review of earlier studies on the dairy development impact on rural poor in India.

Chapter four describes the agro-economic features of Chittoor district and its regional variations, livestock and dairy development programmes, and analysis of regional variations in milk procurement, milk cooperatives and their concentration in the three regions of the district.

Chapter five is devoted to the analysis of primary data. It deals with the socio-economic conditions of agricultural labourers, income and employment generation in dairying and poverty dimensions of agricultural labourers in Chittoor district. Here the effect of Operation Flood programme as an anti poverty measure is presented.

The concluding part of the study is presented in Chapter six which gives overall summary and findings keeping in view the various objectives of this study.

2

NATURE AND DIMENSIONS OF RURAL POVERTY

Most of the people in the World are poor, so if we know the economics of being poor we know much of the Economics that really matters.

—*Theodore W. Shultz, 1979*

2.1 Introduction

Poverty is a multi-dimensional concept[1]. It refers to the lack of access to a set of minimum needs for living. Minimum needs include food, water, housing, clothing, education and health facilities and many other related basic needs. Among all, the requirement of food has the highest priority. The definition of poverty line being used in the context of the plan corresponds to an income/expenditure with which an individual when left to himself will meet the caloric need for active and healthy life[2].

The poor are a mixed group, some cope reasonably well; others are on the margin of survival. Their well-being can fluctuate widely: A good crop with a new seed, or the chance to work on a nearby road project, may push a poor farm family's income and on the other two years of inadequate rain or about a few days of illness may cost them their land or their livestock - a degree of vulnerability that understandably makes for caution and aversion to risk[3].

The poor have other things in common, apart from their extremely low incomes. A disproportionate number of them - perhaps two in five - are children under 10, mainly in large families. More than three-quarters of them live in (often very remote) rural areas, the rest in urban slums - but almost all in very crowded conditions. Many poor families own a small piece of land, some animals or some tools[4]. But both they and other poor people live mainly by working long hours - men, women and children alike - as farmers, vendors and artisans, or hired workers.

They consume as much as four-fifths of their income as food. The result is a monotonous, limited diet of cereals, yams or cassava - with a few vegetables and in some places a little fish or meat. Many of them are malnourished to the point where their ability to work hard is reduced, the physical and mental development of their children is impaired, and their resistance to infections is low[5].

(a) Poverty Concept and Measurement

The concept of poverty is as old as society. But the heightened awareness of its macro dimensions, roots and remedies in the context of economic development is of recent origin. In the past the explanation for its existence was sought in terms of individual deficiencies of character and productive skills. Though it may be true to a limited extent in explaining instances of individual poverty, it failed in the face of massive and continuing poverty witnessed all over the developing world. As a consequence the need for examining the phenomenon as a process in contrast to its theorization as rooted in the individual has become immanent[6]. The phenomenon has thus come to be viewed in terms of its social origin[7] and causation rather than in terms of individual inhibitions and inadequacies. And the discriminating nature of the process of development has come to be understood in terms of the bargaining strength of different socio-economic groups which participate in the process; as a consequence, there is increased recognition and wider acceptance that accelerated growth may not by itself solve the unemployment and poverty problems of densely populated countries. Therefore, there is a clear need to understand the nature of poverty in varied dimensions. One of the pre-requisites for incorporating the eradication of poverty, as an object in the plan process, is measurement and identification of the poor.

(b) Absolute and Relative Poverty

Poverty has always had several but not entirely separable meanings and is defined according to the conventions of society in which it occurs[8]. Yet it can be viewed from varied angles for purpose of analysis.

One may draw a distinction between: 'Primary' and 'Secondary' poverty as enunciated by Rowntree in his pioneering studies or we may reckon it in terms of absolute and relative poverty. Rowntree defined that: Families whose total earnings are insufficient to obtain the minimum necessaries for the maintenance of merely physical efficiency as being in primary poverty[9]." Relying on Atwaters works bearing on the impact of nutritional intakes on the maintenance of body weight of persons, he estimated the average nutritional needs of adults and children, translated these needs into quantities of different foods and hence into the cash equivalent of these foods[10]. To these costs he added minimum sum of clothing, fuel and other expenses according to the size of family. Rent was treated as an unavoidable addition to this sum and was counted in full. A family was, therefore, regarded as being in poverty if its income minus rent fell short of the poverty line.

He further defined secondary poverty as: "Families whose total earnings would be sufficient for the maintenance of merely physical efficiency (at primary level) were it not that some portion of it absorbed by other expenditure either useful or wasteful[11]. Rowntree's use of the concept of secondary poverty has enriched the notion of poverty by indicating that living in a state of poverty was entirely a matter of income[12].

Absolute standards for poverty emphasize subsistence and economic insufficiency as the frame of reference for poverty.

According to Mr.Robert Mc.Namera, the former President of World Bank, "Absolute poverty is a condition of life so degraded by disease, illiteracy, malnutrition, and squalor as to deny its victims basic human necessities ...... a condition of life so limited as to prevent realization of the genes with which one is born, a condition of life so degrading as to insult human dignity and yet a condition of life so common as to be the lot of some 40 per cent of the people of developing countries[13]".

Relative standards stress economic inequality as the primary indicator of poverty. "Relative poor were those whose average income was less than one-third of the national average"[14]. While the concept of absolute poverty approximates to the primary category of Rowntree, his secondary poverty could be viewed as a component of the relative type[15].

2.2 Global Poverty : An Outlook

The poverty in the world today must be mainly understood in an absolute sense[16]. The Third World with 70 per cent of the World population, subsists on only 20 per cent of the World Income and even this meager income is so maldistributed internally as to leave the bulk of its population in abject poverty[17]. The I.L.O. estimated the number of poor in the Third World as follows:

Table-2.1 represents an attempt to assess these numbers in relation to certain criteria[18]. It is suggested that in 1972 some 1200 million people in the developing market economics (67 per cent of their population were seriously poor and 700 million (39 per cent) were distitute and suffering from severe malnutrition. By each of the standards, the proportion of poor in total population is greater in Asia as 71 per cent of the total population is found seriously poor.

The World Bank in 1980 estimated that in developing countries alone nearly 715 million human-beings will be living in absolute poverty by 1985. While their number would probably decline to 600 million at the end of the century, given these optimistic estimates, human beings falling below the absolute poverty line in developing countries would decline from 37 per cent of total world population to 27 per cent in 1985 and may further decline to 17 per cent by 2000 A.D. But Human Development Report 1991[19] estimated that in 1990 there are 1200 million poor in the world of which 860 million poor are in 10 developing countries alone.

Table 2.1

Estimated Number of People in Developing Market-Economies Living in Poverty, 1972*

Region	*Millions of Population*			*Percentage of Population*	
	Total Population	*Seriously poor*	*Distitutes*	*Seriously poor*	*Distitute*
Asia	1,196	853	499	71	42
Africa	345	239	134	69	39
Latin America	274	118	73	43	27
Total	1,815	1,210	706	67	39

* Excluding developing countries in Europe and Oceania with a total population of about 25 million.

Source: ILO, Employment, Growth and Basic Needs: A One World Problem, p. 22.

Table 2.2

Projected Level of Absolute Poverty 1975-2000 AD

(in millions)

	1975	*1985*	*2000*
Low income countries	630	575	540
Middle income countries	140	140	60
All Developing countries	770	715	600

Source: World Bank Annual Report, Quoted in Economic Times, August, 12, 1980.

2.2.1 Extent of Global Rural Poverty

The bulk of the World's absolute poor, about 85 per cent live in rural areas, where for the foreseeable future the majority of them will have to continue to search for income and employment[20]. The urgency of the problem compounded mostly in South Asia and Africa. The majority of the rural poor are agricultural producers with small holdings, most of whom have had little or no access to government services, technical assistance or source of credit. It is being increasingly recognised taht this "small farmer" group constitutes a resource base for major agricultural programmes so that the increasing productivity of small farmers can provide a significant boost to national economic growth as well as improved income distribution within a country.

In addition, however, the rural poor also include large number of the landless as well as tenants or share croppers with precarious land tenure arrangements. The latter group may cultivate sizeable agricultural areas, particularly in countries where income distribution is highly uneven, and where few efforts have been made to redistribute land holdings. For these groups the link between increasing productivity and increasing incomes is much less direct and it has proved much more difficult to reach them through Government programmes. Even more difficult to reach are the poor without land who might seek permanent or temporary-employment elsewhere. In several densely populated countries, the group of poor is rapidly expanding. It also forms the largest group of potential migrants to the urban areas.

Between 25 to (and) 35 per cent of the rural population in developing countries is believed to be primarily depending on non-farm employment and the income of many others also substantially augmented by non-farm work. Rural non-farm activities such as village industries, farm equipment repair shops, carpentry and produce marketing are a vital element in any programme to develop the rural areas that is to supply services and inputs which are essential for increasing agricultural productivity. Experience shows that as agricultural production expands through more intensive cultivation and to use of more advanced technology non-farm activities tend to expand at an even higher rate. Thus, there is general recognition that the poor are disproportionately located in rural areas and are engaged in agriculture or allied rural occupations[21]. This directs attention to the importance of the production of food and other farm products as the major source of income- monetary and subsistence for the bulk of the population in most developing countries.

2.2.2 Nature of Rural Poverty

One way of analysing rural poverty or deprivation is in terms of five interlocking dimensions[22].

(a) Poverty proper (lack of assets and lack of flows of food and cash);

(b) Physical weakness (reflected in lower body weights and greater seasonal variations in those weights);

(c) Vulnerability to contingencies (to irreversible ratchets of impoverishment - the mortgage or scale of assets or the incurring of debts, because of sickness, famine, disaster, dowry, bride wealth and other costs);

(d) Powerlessness (both political and in terms of control of events and relationships) and;

(e) Isolation.

All the five facts contribute to the integrated nature of rural poverty; and the list does not include many other influences - international, intra-national, within rural society- which perpetuate and deepen poverty, in which they live and any effort made in this regard depends both on national and international commitment to the policies chosen.

2.2.3 Characteristics of the Rural Poor[23]

(a) Dependence on Agriculture for a Livelihood

Labour Surveys in Africa and Asia show that agricultural employment is the principal occupation for 75 to 80 per cent of the rural population; with partial exception of some relatively advanced countries and areas close to cities, almost every one has some connection with agriculture. There is a correspondingly thin scatter of jobs in rural industry, commerce, transport and services (including educational and administrative services). Though agriculture provides most of the work and incomes in rural areas, non-agricultural activities are important supplementary sources of income for rural households. A shortage of remunerative work opportunities off the farm during the slack season may greatly increase the poverty of those whose holdings are too small or too unproductive to provide an adequate livelihood. The poorest income groups in rural areas - the landless and near landless - often depend on activities which may contribute only indirectly to higher agricultural output.

(b) Compounding Effects of Natural Calamities

There are times - typically after floods or drought have ruined the harvest — when virtually the entire population of a large area is seriously affected. An important region where such situation is common is represented by the so-called "drought prone areas" of India, which cover about 600,000 Sq.Km. and have a population of approximately 66 million. The bulk of this population is engaged in a perennial struggle to meet subsistence needs in a generally harsh environment. Within this broad zone, drought has occurred in three or four years out of every ten with good and bad years tending to cluster together. The succession of drought years has severely affected the harvest, and has resulted in absolute poverty for more than three-fourths of the total population of the zone.

(c) Small and Fragmented Holdings

Incomes at the farm level are determined by a host of factors that include the quantity and quality of inputs such as land, labour and water, the technology used, the prices received for outputs and prices paid for inputs. Thus, an irrigated farm of one hectare using high yielding varieties of paddy and fertilizer can generate double the income of the same area farmed by traditional methods. One hectare devoted to tea can yield an income seven times as great as when it is used for maize. Studies indicate that most of the small holdings in Asia,

Africa and Latin America are used for traditional low yielding subsistence production. These studies also indicate that very few farms of less than two hectares of arable land, producing traditional crops generate incomes above the poverty line.

(d) Tenants and Share Croppers

Most of the tenants and sharecroppers in poorer countries share their output with land owners and often operate under insecure tenancies. Other things being equal, tenants incomes will be even lower than those of the small operator-owners, and the amount of land required for an income above the poverty line is correspondingly larger.

(e) Landless and Other Rural Workers

Most workers in rural areas are classified as self-employed or family workers, but the poorest farm households also derive a significant proportion of their income from wage employment in agricultural and non-agricultural activities. There is a large and growing group of landless and near landless workers - heavily concentrated in those Asian countries with the largest concentration of the poor. Most of the landless work... irregularly, often on a seasonal basis; many work only when labour requirements are at a peak. Wage rates are extremely low. Not all farm workers are so badly off, some workers in plantations and in enclave enterprises have incomes that place them above the poverty line. In the main, however, agricultural workers and the landless whose employment is seasonal are among the poorest members of the country.

2.2.4 World Bank and the Anti-Poverty Strategy

By recognising the fact that "poverty any where constitutes a danger to prosperity every where", the focus of national and international efforts including that of World Bank was to be directed during the 1970's towards increasing the productivity of the poor. It was recognised that welfare programmes without corresponding increase in productivity of recipients could be short lived and counter productive. It was emphasised that to the extent that the poor possessed some tangible assets, however, meagre (small farm, cottage industry, etc.) national and international action should focus on helping them to become more productive through better access to credit, extension assistance, and productive inputs such as fertilizer and improved seeds. The Bank also recognized the need to expand public services such as education, health care, water supply and public transportation. The direct attack on mass poverty has also been broadened by the World Bank to include those who have no tangible assets, or those cannot easily be reached by simply expanding existing public services. World Bank lending for Rural Development has increased from a negligible proportion ten years ago to over 20 per cent of total lending today[24]. The Bank also has increasingly designed "New Style Projects" with the objective of directly benefiting the poor people. A minimum objective of these new style projects is atleast 51 per cent of their beneficiaries should fall with in target group constituting the bottom 40 per cent of the population. In fact actual experience so far shows that coverage has been far higher. As per World Development Report, 1980, in 1977, 69 per cent of the beneficiaries of the new style rural development projects were in the poverty target groups.

(a) World Development Report 1990 Recommendations

Further, the 1990 World Development Report recommended a two part approach to reduce poverty. The first part focuses on generating economic growth by employing the poor in labour intensive activities. The second port focuses on ensuring that the poor have access to basic social services, such as primary health care, basic education and family planning.

Based on World Development Reports' findings, World Bank officials have formulated an approach for ensuring that the World Development Reports' recommendations are put into practice. Stressing that, the objective is to ensure development programmes supported by the Bank are clearly generated to a reduction of poverty, the new approach calls for the Bank to work with member countries to assess the impact of their economic policies on the poor. Periodic review of the links between economic growth and poverty reduction in each borrowing country would be carried out under the new approach.

However, the World Bank effort alone to eradicate poverty is not enough. This requires intensive coordination at national, regional and local levels[25]. Explicit concern for the problem of poverty in developing countries - the problem of poor people and not merely concern with the poor countries - has become an ubiquitous theme in the development literature.

2.2.5 Indian Poverty in World Perspective

The attention of multilateral agencies is mainly focused on the Asian countries which amount for three-fourth of the Third World Population living in absolute poverty. The Table 2.3 presents the ten developing countries with highest number of poor people (1990). These ten countries accounted 72 per cent of total world's poor. It is sad to note that 410 million poor or 34 per cent of world poor are in India. In other words more than one-third of the world poor are in India alone. Hence,

Table 2.3
The Ten Developing Countries with Highest Number of Poor People (1990)

S.No.	*Country*	*Number of poor (million)*	*Poor as percentage to world poor*
1.	India	410	34.2
2.	China	120	9.9
3.	Bangladesh	99	8.3
4.	Indonesia	70	5.8
5.	Pakistan	37	3.1
6.	Philippines	36	3.0
7.	Brazil	33	2.8
8.	Ethiopia	30	2.5
9.	Myanmar	17	1.4
10.	Thailand	17	1.4
	Total	**869**	**72.4**

Source: Human Development Report 1992, UNDP, p. 42.

no programme for successful fight against poverty in the world be said to have succeeded, if the problem of poverty is not successfully tackled in India[26].

Therefore there is a need to understand the nature of poverty in varied dimensions and to frame suitable policies to overcome this problem. In India poverty studies have began with the writings of Dadabhai Nauroji in 19th century. After independence there is a revival of interest on the problem of poverty and the recent studies are concentrated with the magnitude and characteristics of the poor but most of these studies are macro level studies based on N.S.S. data and assume the value of food for a caloric intake of 2,250 for rural people and 2,100 for urban as the basis as per the recommendations of Indian Council of Medical Research (1959).

2.3 Review of Literature on Indian Poverty

(a) Dandekar V.M. and Rath N, estimate

Dandekar and Rath by using the National Sample Survey (NSS) data estimated private consumer expenditure at rural and urban households relating to 1960-61 and on the basis of the distribution of the expenditure, they determined the level of poverty. They found that an annual per capita expenditure of Rs.180 was required in rural areas as against Rs.270 in urban areas to give a diet adequate in respect of Calories (2,250 calories required per day).

On this basis, the authors estimated, the constant proportion of about 40 per cent of the rural population and about 50 per cent of urban population to lie below the desirable minimum both in 1960-61 and 1967-68. But in absolute terms rural poor increased from 135 million to 166 million and urban poor from 42 to 49 million.

(b) B.S. Minhas Estimate

B.S.Minhas attempted to determine the number of people falling below the poverty line between 1957-58 and 1967-68 on the basis of N.S.S. data relating to private consumption expenditure. In estimating poverty, he used two standards, namely Rs.240 as recommended by a working group set up by the Planning Commission in 1962 and Rs.200 percapita annual consumption expenditure at 1961-62 prices considering somewhat lower level for rural areas. If Rs.240 is taken as the minimum level of living, people below poverty line come down from 215 to 210 million i.e., 65 per cent to 50.6 per cent in between 1957-58 and 1967-68. If Rs.200 is taken as the minimum level of living, then the number of people below the poverty line works out to be 173 million (52.4 per cent) in 1956-57 to 154 (37 per cent) in 1967-68. The number of people below poverty line seems to have fallen in good harvest years, but shot up again in bad years. However, there has been a steady decline in the proportion of people below the poverty line.

According to his study a large bulk of the rural poor belong to:

(a) Agricultural labour households without land, which formed 58 to 61 per cent of all agricultural labour households between 1956-57 and 1963-64.

(b) Other labour households without land.

(c) Agricultural Labour Households with land, which formed 42 to 39 per cent of all agricultural labour households between 1956-57 and 1963-64 and;

(d) All small land operators, operating holdings below 5 acres in size.

In addition to these studies, about Indian poverty, various studies of different scholars, and institutions are summarised in Table 2.4.

Various studies listed in Table 2.4 have estimated the percentage of rural population below the poverty line using different parameters. The proportion of population below poverty line varies from 35 per cent according to De-costa to 70 per cent as per Ojha during 1960's. The estimates of other studies lie in between these two extremes. During 1970's the percentage of population below poverty line varied between 41 per cent according to Ahluwalia and 51 per cent as per

NIRD and other estimates stand in between these two estimates.

Table-2.4
Comparative Statement Showing Different Estimates of Rural Poverty in India

Sl. No.	*Year*	*Organisational research*	*Estimated No. of poor (millions)*	*Percentage of rural population below poverty line*	*Parameters of poverty*
1	2	3	4	5	6
1.	1960-61	V.M. Dandekar and N.Rath	135.0	40.0	Rs.180 Pc, c.e, p.a at 1960-61 prices yielding a minimum of 2250 calories per day.
		Ahluwalia	152.0	42.0	Rs.180 Pc, c.e, p.a. at 1960-61 prices
		Vaidyanathan	213.5	59.5	Rs.240 Pc, c.e, p.a. at 1960-61 prices
		Ojha	184.2	51.8	Rs.216 Pc, c.e, p.a. at 1960-61 prices
2.	1961-62	Ahluwalia	157.0	42.3	Rs.180 Pc, c.e, p.a. at 1960-61 prices
3.	1962-63	NIRD	166.0	44.9	The regression equation between NDP from agriculture and Ahluwalia time series estimate of incidence of poverty.
4.	1963-64	EPW De Costa	161.8	34.6	Three classifications: Destitutes, severe destitutes and the poor based on minimum per capita expenditure per annum.
		B.S.Minhas	221.0	57.8	Two alternative levels of Rs..240 and Rs.200 per capita annual consumption expenditure at 1960-61 prices.

1	2	3	4	5	6
		Ahluwalia	189.0	49.1	Above mentioned criterion.
5.	1964-65	Vaidyanathan	235.7	60.0	As mentioned ąbove (Rs.240, Pc, c.e. p.a)
		Bardhan	174.4	51.6	Rs.180 Pc, c.e, p.a. at 1960-61 prices
		Ahluwalia	198.0	50.4	Above mentioned criterion.
6.	1965-66	Ahluwalia	205.0	51.0	Above mentioned criterion.
7.	1966-67	Ahluwalia	235.0	57.4	Above mentioned criterion.
8.	1967-68	Ahluwalia	241.0	57.9	Above mentioned criterion.
		Dandekar and Rath	164.4	40.0	Above mentioned criterion.
		Vidyanathan	166.4	67.8	Above mentioned criterion.
		Minhas	210.0	50.6	Rs.240, P.c; c.e, p.a.
		Ojha	289.0	70.0	Estimates of minimum-desirable income i.e., Rs.216 to Rs.480 p.a.
9.	1968-69	Ahluwalia	227.0	53.5	Above mentioned criterion.
10.	1969-70	AF ICCI	218.3	41.2	Rs.240 P.c, c.e, p.a.. at 1960-61 Prices, Rs.444 p.c.c.e, p.a. at 1969-70 prices.
		NIRD	196.0	46.2	Earlier mentioned criterion.
11.	1970-71	NIRD	217.0	49.1	Earlier mentioned criterion.
	1971	IIPO	198.9	45.0	Rs.336 p.c., c.e., p.a.
12.	1971-72	NIRD	183.0	41.5	Earlier mentioned criterion.
		Ahluwalia	180.9	41.2	Earlier mentioned criterion.
13.	1972-73	NIRD	212.0	47.2	Earlier mentioned criterion.
		Ahluwalia	191.9	43.1	Earlier mentioned criterion.
14.	1973-74	Ahluwalia	221.0	47.6	Earlier mentioned criterion.
		IIPO	208.0	44.8	Rs.516 p.c., c.e., p.a.,

1	2	3	4	5	6
15.	1974-75	NIRD	232.0	50.1	Earlier mentioned criterion.
16.	1975-76	NIRD	225.0	47.7	Earlier mentioned criterion.
17.	1976-77	NIRD	216.0	45.2	Earlier mentioned criterion.
18.	1977-78	IIPO	246.4	50.8	Rs.780 p.c, c.e, p.a (2400 calories p.c. per day)
19.	1983	World Bank	252	44.9	Rs.89 at 1983-84 prices
20.	1988	World Bank	252	41.7	Rs.89 at 1983-84 prices
21.	1987-88	Minhas Jain and Tendulkar	284	44.8	Rs.122.6 at current prices.

Note : NIRD : National Institute of Rural Development

IIPO: Indian Institute of Public Opinion

P.c. : Per capita
c.e. : Consumer expenditure
p.a. : Per annum

Source :

1. Dandekar, V.M. and N.Rath; Poverty in India, Indian School of Political Economy, Poona, 1970.
2. Ahluwalia, M.S., Rural Poverty and Agricultural Performance in India, The Journal of Development India, No.3, Vol.14, April, 1978.
3. Vaidyanathan, A.; "Some Aspects of Inequalities in Living Standards in Rural Area", Sankhya, Vol.36 (1974), Series C, Part 2 and 4.
4. Minhas, B.S.; "Rural Poverty, Land Redistribution and Development Strategy: Facts", Sankhya, Vol.36 (1974), Series C, Part 2 and 4.
5. Bardhan, P.K., "On the Incidence of Poverty in Rural India in Sixties", Sankhya, Ibid.
6. Ojha, P.D.; "A Configuration of Indian Poverty: Incidence and Levels of Living", Reserve Bank of India Bulletin, Vol.24, 1970.
7. Balakrishna, S. and Ghosh, P.K. "Poverty line Redefined and Confirmed", Behavioural Sciences and Rural Development, Vol.3, No.1, January, 1980.
8. Balakrishna, S.; Incidence of Rural Poverty in Recent years, Behavioural Sciences and Rural Development, Vol.3, No.1, January, 1980.

9. Indian Institute of Public Opinion (1978-79), The Measurement of Depreciation by Degrees of Distinction in Indian State 1973-74, Quarterly Economic Report, Vol.XXIV, No.1, 93, Oct. 1978/ July, 1979.

10. World Bank (1989), India: Poverty, Employment and Social services.

11. Minhas B.S., Jain L.R., Tendulkar, S.D.; Declining Incidence of Poverty in 1980's, EPW, July 6-13, 1991.

Since poverty parameters differ from one study to another, poverty trends estimated by different studies can be viewed independently.

(a) Ahluwalia presented an increasing trend from 42 per cent to 58 per cent in between 1961-62 and 1967-68 and then decreasing trend to 48 per cent by 1973-74.

(b) NIRD estimates also denote an increasing trend of poverty from 45 per cent to 50 per cent during 1962-63 and 1974-75 after that declined to 45 per cent in 1976-77.

(c) Indian Institute of Public Opinion estimates realises a nominal decrease from 45 per cent to 44.8 per cent in between 1971 and 1973-74 and further has gone up to 51 per cent in 1977-78.

(d) The World Bank estimated that rural poor in India are 252 millions in 1983 as well as in 1988, however, in relative terms rural poverty has decreased from 45 per cent to 42 per cent.

(e) But as per Minhas *et al.*, estimate in 1987-88 there are 284 million rural poor accounts to 45 per cent of total population in India.

(c) Official Poverty Estimates

Since alleviation of poverty and unemployment continue to be the longrun objective of economic and social development in India, the Planning Commission has been preparing estimates of the proportion and number of poor in the country. Such estimates were prepared for 1972-73, 1977-78, 1983-84, 1987-88 and 1999-2000. These were based on the concept of poverty line and data on household expenditure obtained through National Sample Survey Rounds. Following the recommendations of the Task Force on Projection of Minimum Needs and Effective Consumption Demand (1979), the poverty line was defined as the per capita monthly expenditure needed to obtain the consumption basket corresponding to the calorie norms of 2400 per capita per day in rural areas and 2100 per capita in urban areas in the base year 1973-74[27]. The poverty line defined was Rs.49.10 for rural areas and Rs.56.60 for urban areas per month. The same poverty line was updated for subsequent years using suitable indicators of change in cost of living.

Table 2.5
Percentage of Population Living Below the Poverty Line

Area	*1972-73*	*1977-78*	*1983-84*	*1987-88*	*1999-2000*
Rural	54.1	51.2	40.4	33.4	27.1
Urban	41.2	38.2	28.1	20.1	23.6
Combined	51.5	48.3	37.4	29.9	26.1

Source: Govt. of India, **Economic Survey, 1993-94** and 2002-2003, Ministry of Finance, Economic Division, New Delhi, p.148 and 213 respectively.

As shown in Table 2.5, the per cent percentage of population living below the poverty line both rural and urban has continuously declined since 1972-73 to 1999-2000.

In view of the methodological issues raised in respect of the estimates on poverty and also poverty alleviation being an objective of economic and social development, the Planning Commission constituted an Expert Group in September 1989 to consider methodology and computational aspects of estimation of proportion and number of poor in the country. The Expert Group, while retaining the concept of poverty line as recommended by the Task Force, suggested change in the price deflator to update the poverty line for use in later years. It suggested use of State specific price indices which can reflect the changes in cost of consumption basket of the people around the poverty line. It relied exclusively on the National Sample Survey data on consumption expenditure to assess the incidence of poverty without adjusting the NSS consumption to that obtained from macro-aggregates of the national accounts. The estimates of percentage of population living below the poverty line arrived at by the Expert Group are presented in Table 2.6.

Table 2.6
Percentage of Population Living Below the Poverty Line - Expert Group Estimates

Area	*1973-74*	*1977-78*	*1983-84*	*1987-88*
Rural	56.4	53.1	45.6	39.1
Urban	49.2	47.4	42.2	40.1
Combined	54.9	51.8	44.8	39.3

Source: 1. Govt. of India, Planning Commission, **Report of the Expert Group on Estimation of Proportion and Number of Poor,** July 1993.

2. Govt. of India, **Economic Survey, 1993-94,** Ministry of Finance, Economic Division, New Delhi, p. 184.

The report of the Expert Group which was submitted in July 1993 was released by the Planning Commission. The Expert Group poverty estimates are higher than Planning Commission estimates but it also confirm a study decline in the proportion of population living below the poverty line since 1973-74. Yet a substantially high proportion of people continue to be living below the poverty line.

(d) ICRISAT Findings (World Development Report 1990, Oxford University Press, p. 35).

International Crop Research Institute for Semi Arid Tropics (ICRISAT) based in Hyderabad, India collected data about the income and consumption of 211 agricultural households in Central India between 1975 and 1983 where drought conditions are common. According to this study percentage of households deemed to be poor fluctuating over time around a generally downward trend from 64 per cent at the beginning of the period to a low of 41 per cent in 1982; the average proportion of poor was 50 per cent.

In this study for each year the poor are divided into those who were poor in the previous period and those who were not and the same is done for the non-poor. On average 84 per cent of the poor at each date had been poor in the previous period. Of the non-poor, 75 per cent had been non-poor in the previous period, and 25 per cent had moved out of poverty.

Only about 12 per cent of households were never poor during the nine years (not necessarily consecutive). At the other extreme, 44 per cent were poor for six or more years, and 19 per cent were poor in every year. Thus most households in these villages do experience poverty at one time or another.

2.4 Poverty of Agricultural Labour Households in India

(a) Incidence of Poverty Among Agricultural Labour Households (1956-57)

V.M.Dandekar and N.Rath (1971) analysed the incidence of poverty among agricultural labour households for the year 1956-57 based on the Eleventh and Twelfth Rounds of National Sample Survey (NSS) data which covered over the period from August 1956 to August 1957. The percentage distribution of agricultural labor households according to their annual per capita consumption expenditure for the year 1956-57 is given for the six population zones of the country (Table 2.7).

The accepted desirable minimum consumption in rural areas is Rs.180 per capita per annum at 1960-61 prices and this is approximately equal to Rs.150 per capita per annum at 1956-57 prices[28]. Hence it will be seen that about 57 per cent of the agricultural labour households lived below the minimum. The incidence of poverty among the agricultural labour households is again some what different in different regions (See Table 2.7). To judge, what portion of rural poverty is due to agricultural labour households, the proportion of agricultural labour households among rural households living at different levels of per capita annual consumer expenditure is presented in Table 2.8.

Table 2.7
Percentage Distribution of Agricultural Labour Households by Annual Per Capita Consumption Expenditure (1956-57)

Annual per capita consumption Expenditure (Rs.)	*North India*	*East India*	*South India*	*West India*	*Central India*	*North west*	*All India*
Upto 100	22.77	22.64	29.96	23.98	33.13	11.12	25.88
101-150	33.92	28.92	29.41	34.97	35.52	25.00	31.05
151-200	19.25	21.67	20.23	19.19	16.34	22.53	19.96
Above 200	19.06	26.77	20.40	22.76	15.01	41.35	23.11
Total	100	100	100	100	100	100	100

Source: Dandekar, V.M. and Rath, N. (1970), Poverty in India, The Ford Foundation, New Delhi, p. 21.

Table 2.8
Proportion (Percentage) of Agricultural Labour Households Among Rural Households at Different Levels of Consumer Expenditure (1956-57)

Annual per capita consumption Expenditure (Rs.)	*North India*	*East India*	*South India*	*West India*	*Central India*	*North west*	*All India*
Upto 100	36.28	43.87	49.21	42.07	44.87	15.51	41.91
101-150	22.15	35.25	40.26	34.85	33.69	11.69	31.90
151-200	15.50	29.77	32.26	22.75	22.10	9.38	24.19
Above 200	8.13	16.35	19.44	12.29	13.73	5.80	13.94
Total	17.00	27.03	33.16	23.57	27.58	8.04	24.55

Source: Dandekar, V.M. and Rath, N. (1970), Ibid., p. 22.

It will be seen that among rural households living at less than Rs.100 per capita per annum agricultural labour households constituted more than 40 per cent. In South India about half of the households living at this level were agricultural labour households. Among the rural households with annual per capita consumer expenditure between Rs.101-150, agricultural labour households in India constituted nearly one-third. In South India, they constituted over 40 per cent of the rural households living at this level. Thus the rural poverty at the lowest level is largely accounted for by the agricultural labour households. Nevertheless, even at this level they (agricultural labourers) do not account for more than half of the poor[29].

(b) Incidence of Poverty Among Agricultural Labour Households (1977-78)

S.Mahendra Dev[30] estimated the incidence of poverty for the year 1977-78 by making use of NSS 32nd Round data on employment and income of agricultural labour households, self-employed in agricultural occupations, other labour households and other rural households on the basis of head count ratio at the state level. He has taken Rs.180 per capita per year at 1960-61 prices as poverty line like Dandekar and Rath.

In 1977-78, the incidence of poverty of all households in India is 37 per cent (Table 2.9). As expected poverty turns out to be the highest among agricultural labour households in India with 56 per cent followed by other labour households; self-employed in non-agriculture households/ self-employed in agricultural households and other rural households. The State level analysis denotes that the incidence of poverty in all states is highest only among agricultural labour households though there are variations from state to state.

The composition of different categories of households to the poverty households is presented in Table 2.10. In India agricultural labour households turn out to be the single largest segment of poverty households (45 per cent) followed by self employed households in agricultural occupations. It is also true in almost all the states except Assam, Madhya Pradesh, Rajastan and Uttar Pradesh. In India as well as in Andhra

Pradesh about 80 per cent of poverty households constituted by agricultural labour households and self-employed in agricultural occupations. In Andhra Pradesh though incidence of poverty is 37 per cent among agricultural labour households and these (agricultural labourer) households constituted about 55 per cent of rural households.

Table 2.9
Incidence of Poverty by Household Type 1977-78

	Agricultural Labour households	*Self-employed in agriculture*	*Self employed in non-agriculture*	*Other labour house holds*	*Other house holds*	*Total*
Andhra Pradesh	36.91	20.86	24.51	23.71	20.05	28.10
Assam	55.54	27.23	26.31	53.29	23.70	35.16
Bihar	72.08	37.76	52.24	50.80	41.47	52.51
Gujarat	45.87	22.92	18.38	22.19	9.15	28.89
Haryana	33.39	10.49	26.53	3.74	1.37	24.72
Karnataka	54.54	26.86	35.48	37.52	22.16	38.69
Kerala	54.79	23.10	35.59	18.51	2.63	36.52
Madhya Pradesh	63.41	42.47	47.28	48.73	22.39	47.94
Maharasthra	64.12	36.05	45.51	45.42	25.06	47.46
Orissa	77.10	45.55	54.28	61.62	35.88	58.12
Punjab	19.15	3.78	12.14	16.51	7.87	9.93
Rajasthan	38.95	20.22	22.83	25.78	11.40	22.14
Tamil Nadu	58.02	33.22	39.43	33.41	24.53	43.23
Uttar Pradesh	53.77	28.88	40.49	37.13	24.86	34.93
West Bengal	81.13	45.96	57.84	53.34	41.90	60.26
All India	55.90	28.00	35.71	36.34	22.00	37.33

Source: Basic Data compiled from NSS 32nd Round on Employment and Unemployment, **National Sample Survey Organisation**, Ministry of Planning, Cabinet Secretariat, Govt. of India, New Delhi, 1981.

As quoted in Mahendra Dev, Ibid., (1988), p. 17.

Table 2.10
Percentage Share of Households Types in All Rural Households Below the Poverty Line 1977-78

	Agricultural Labour households	*Self-employed in agriculture*	*Rest of the house holds*	*Total house holds*
Andhra Pradesh	54.44	24.72	20.84	100.00
Assam	26.85	44.13	29.02	100.00
Bihar	49.52	31.04	19.44	100.00
Gujarat	49.36	39.54	11.10	100.00
Haryana	32.49	30.52	36.99	100.00
Karnataka	53.47	28.27	18.26	100.00
Kerala	40.52	17.96	41.52	100.00
Madhya Pradesh	39.91	52.11	7.98	100.00
Maharasthra	52.21	30.25	17.54	100.00
Orissa	49.23	33.10	17.67	100.00
Punjab	46.41	16.92	36.67	100.00
Rajasthan	17.60	61.39	21.06	100.00
Tamil Nadu	52.81	23.29	23.90	100.00
Uttar Pradesh	27.88	48.57	23.55	100.00
West Bengal	48.18	26.93	24.89	100.00
All India	44.74	34.58	20.63	100.00

Source: Ibid.

Table 2.11
Percentage of Agricultural Labour Households Below the Poverty Line (India)

Year	*Per cent of Household*
1956-57	57.00[1]
1977-78	55.90[2]

Source: 1. Dandekar, V.M. and Rath, N., Op.Cit., p. 20.
2. As in Table 2.9.

As shown in the Table 2.11 Dandekar and Rath (1970) as well as Mahendra Dev (1988) estimated that 57 and 56 per cent of agricultural labour households are in poverty in 1956-57 and 1977-78 respectively. Whereas almost the same percentage of agricultural labour households are below the poverty level in both the years on one hand and on the other the total rural households as well as the percentage of agricultural labour households among poor rural households increased, naturally the percentage share of agricultural labour households among poor rural households increased. The Rural Labour Enquires reveal that during 1964-65 and 1983 the number of rural households increased from 70.4 million to 100.5 million on one hand and on the other the percentage of agricultural labour households to rural households increased from 21.8 per cent to 30.7 per cent in the same period. This tendency confirms that the percentage of agricultural labour among rural poor has been increasing irrespective of decreasing (tendency) rural poverty in India.

Hence, in India poverty elimination cannot be realised without uplifting the poor agricultural labourers.

2.5 Public Policy and the Rural Poor in India

As the decade of sixties drew to a close, it becomes increasingly clear that the benefits of rapid growth that had taken place in several developing countries recently had been very unequally shared[31]. In India, which was passing through the throes of the Green Revolution the overall conclusion of a series of studies in the early seventies was that agricultural growth had made little dent on absolute poverty (defined as the number of persons living below the poverty line) or even relative poverty (their proportion in the total population). It becomes increasingly clear that exclusive reliance could no longer be placed on the trickle down of indirect benefit from growth in the modern highly productive sector, since the linkages with the rest of the economy of the majority poverty groups - landless labour, small and marginal farmers, rural artisans and the urban poor in the informal sector were weak. For the hard core of the poor in the rural areas, in particular more direct measures of income and employment generation were necessary[32].

With these past experience, India through a number of public policies, seeks to intervene positively in the developmental process by stimulating production and ensuring distributive justice. The entire thrust appears to be on improving the quality of life of all the citizens especially to protect the disadvantaged groups by solving their basic problem - poverty.

The policies to attack poverty directly, are broadly of two types[33]: (1) The policies which might be called comprehensive and lead to structural transformation like, land-reforms, ceiling on property touch the ownership of the means of production; (2) Incremental policies which are of a reformative type like reservations, public distributive system; subsidised anti-poverty schemes. These policies are intended to provide some relief to the poorer sections without effecting the basic socio-economic structure of the society.

The Indian Government pursues both types of policies and covers a wide range of socio-economic process touching the life of the community at various points so as to establish a socialistic pattern of society. The general problem of the abolition of poverty has increasingly merged with, and has often become the foundation of the social and political policy of Government[34].

(a) Direct Anti-Poverty Interventions

Since the mid 1970s, the Central and State Governments have launched numerous direct anti-poverty interventions. The important direct interventions launched with the initiative of the Central Government are: (a) Integrated Rural Development Programme; (b) Drought - Prone Area Programme; (c) National Rural Employment Programme; (d) Training of Rural Youth for Self-Employment Guarantee Programme. At State level the notable programmes are: (a) Maharastra's Employment Guarantee Scheme, (b) Public Distribution System in Kerala, Tamil Nadu, Gujarat and Andhra Pradesh (Rs.2/- kilo rice scheme). Thus India is experimenting in many directions to reduce poverty-induced human suffering through various anti-poverty programmes. As a result, the inequality in income distribution, as measured by the concentration ratio of expenditure distribution has go down to a level around 0.18 from the existing level of 0.30 in between 1977-78 and 1983[35] through successful execution of the poverty alleviation programmes stipulated above. This no doubt, would be a big improvement in the distribution of income[36].

(b) Degree of Success in Eradication of Poverty

National Sample Survey Organisation (NSSO) Report on household consumption expenditure provides the distribution of the number of households by expenditure class based on per-capita expenditure. The Report also provides the consumption of different food and non-food items in different expenditure classes. These results are utilised by the Planning Commission for estimation of percentage of persons below poverty line. Draft Sixth Five Year Plan (1980-86) presented two alternative estimates of poverty for the year 1984-85. Accordingly the magnitude of poverty was placed at 279 million (39 per cent) if redistribution measures are not implemented. And this figure is expected to come down.to 215 million (30 per cent) through implementation of redistribution measures.

As shown in the Table 2.12, Sixth Five Year Plan (1980-85) sets the alternative poverty targets - one refers the incidence of poverty without redistributive measures and another refers the incidence of poverty with effective implementation of redistributive measures for 1984-85. The two surveys of National Sample Survey Organisation relate to 1977-78 and 1983 provided the poverty estimates for 1977-78 and 1983-84. In addition, Centre for Monitoring Indian Economy (1992) provided the poverty estimates for the year 1984-85.

Though inequality in consumption expenditure has come down to 0.18 from 0.38 in between 1977-78 and 1983 (See reference 35) as a result of successful execution of poverty alleviation programmes (mostly redistributive in nature) incidence of rural poverty has go down to 40 per cent instead of 30 per cent which is expected to achieve with effective implementation of poverty alleviation programmes.

Table 2.12
Percentage of People Below Poverty Line in India

Year	*Rural*	*Urban*	*Total*
1972-73	(54.09)	(41.22)	(51.49)
1977-78	251.66	51.10	302.76
	(50.82)	(38.19)	(48.13)
1984-85[a]	223.97	55.21	279.18
	(40.47)	(33.71)	(38.93)
1984-85[b]	166.02	49.14	215.16
	(30.00)	(30.00)	(30.00)
1984-85[c]	221.50	49.40	270.90
	(40.40)	(28.10)	(37.40)
1984-85d[d]	222.20	50.50	272.70
	(39.90)	(27.70)	(36.90)
1983-84[e]	253.90	76.90	331.10
	(45.60)	(42.20)	(44.80)

Note:

a. Magnitude of poverty without redistributive measures (Projections).

b. Magnitude of poverty with redistributive measures (projections).

c. NSSO estimates

d. Centre for Monitoring Indian Economy (1992) estimates.

Source:

1. Government of India, **6th Five Year Plan Draft 1980-85**, p. 51.
2. 1983-84 results are based on the NSS Consumer expenditure distribution of 38th Round Survey on consumer expenditure (provisional) quoted in C.H.Hanumantha Rao, *et al.*, (1985), Poverty Eradication in India by the year 2000; Some Macro Economic Implications, **Man and Development**, December, 1985, p.32.
3. Centre for Monitoring Indian Economy 1992, Basic Statistics relating to Indian Economy, Vol.11, **All India Economic Intelligence Service**, Bombay, Table 7-13.
4. Report of the Expert Group on Estimation of Proportion and number of poor. July 1993; Quoted in Economic Survey, 1993-94, Ministry of Finance, Govt. of India, p. 148.

Thus this phenomenon indicates that mere redistributive measures alone cannot solve the incidence of poverty in near future. This underscores the need for rapid growth of output and employment coupled with strengthening of special programmes of poverty alleviation and employment generation. The problem of poverty has to be dealt in the frame work of the strategy of development laying emphasis on those sectors whose growth makes a significant impact on the income levels of the underemployed[37]. One of such sector is dairy industry though which poverty problem can be solved effectively.

2.6 Summary

Poverty is a multi-dimensional concept therefore there is a clear need to understand the nature of poverty in varied dimensions. One of the pre-requisites for incorporating the eradication of poverty is measurement and identification of the poor. One may draw distinction between absolute Poverty and relative poverty. Absolute standards for poverty emphasize subsistance and economic insufficiency as the frame of reference for poverty and relative standards stress economic inequality as the primary indicator of poverty. The problem of poverty is explained and its origin and measurement are traced.

Incidence of poverty is more in rural India when compared to urban India. Through a number of empirical studies show that there is a declining trend in the incidence of poverty in general, it is not true in the case of agricultural labour class. To alleviate poverty both direct and indirect measures are proposed one such suitable measure is dairy industry.

3

DAIRY DEVELOPMENT AND THE RURAL POOR IN INDIA

Dairying is an instrument of Social and Economic Change.

National Commission on Agriculture,
Interim Report on Milk Production (1971)

3.1 IMPORTANCE OF DAIRY IN INDIA

3.1.1 Introduction

The need for promotion of dairying in India arises due to several considerations such as low per capita availability of milk, prevalence of large scale unemployment and under employment, encouraging mixed farming for fuller utilization of farm by-products and wastages and increasing living conditions of rural poor, achieving self sufficiency in the production of milk and milk products and save valuable foreign exchange. In the ultimate analysis the need for dairy development in India arises due to two main reasons which stand out prominently are:

(a) Supply of adequate quantity of milk at reasonable price to urban consumers;

(b) To provide viable subsidiary occupation to unemployed rural poor so as to raise their income earning capacities. Dairy development programme makes these twin objectives coincide.

The National Commission on Agriculture in its interim report of 1971 recommended the "integrated development of all sections of the rural people in the rural areas" and in this contest recommended the intensification of cattle rearing and milk production programmes. These programmes should be "organised on proper scientific lines and it has to be ensured form the initial planning stage itself that the benefits would be spread over all sections of farmers and in particular reach the small and marginal farmers and `agricultural labourers'.[38] Even though the share of agriculture in GDP has been declining, as an index of diversification of the economic base, welcomed, the share of agricultural work-force in total work force is not declining and that the absolute number of people dependent on agriculture for jobs and income is increasing owing to a low absorptive capacity for labour in industry[39]. This calls for expansion of emerging high demand sub-sectors, chiefly livestock and dairying, horticulture, fisheries, poultry and forestry.[40] Fortunately, in India the value of output from livestock is showing an increasing trend. The contribution of livestock to the agricultural sector stands nearly 24 per cent, i.e., next to land and irrigation, livestock is the largest productive asset in rural India.[41]

According to All India Debt and Investment Survey (1981), 73 per cent of the rural households owned livestock and the average value of this asset per reporting household was Rs.2452. The estimated value of livestock holdings of the rural population is placed at Rs.168 billion (Government of India,1986). The contribution of the dairy sub-sector accounts for nearly two-thirds of the total livestock contribution. The track record of the dairy sector is thus impressive by any yardstick. The growth of agricultural sector has been only marginally higher than the growth of population. But the growth of dairy sector has been at an encouraging 5 per cent. This is despite the fact that investment in animal husbandry and dairying during the five year Plans has ranged from 4.6 per cent (Seventh Five Year Plan) to 7 per cent (Third Five Year Plan) of the total investment made in agriculture.[42]

3.1.2 Indian Dairy in Global Perspective

Cattle and buffaloes have been an integral part of crop-livestock system in Indian farm economy for thousands of years. Possessing 273.3 million bovines (1990), India claims the first position in the world, accounting for 51 per cent of the Asian bovine population (530.1 million) and 19.2 per cent of the World Population (1.420 million).[43] Decomposing the total bovine population into cattle and buffaloes also presents a similar picture. India with a cattle population of 197.3 million accounts for nearly 50 per cent of the Asian population 15.4 per cent of World cattle population. With regard to buffalo population the country is placed in a still more comfortable and enviable position, contributing to 53.3 per cent of the World population and 55 per cent of Asia.

Milk has now emerged as the second largest agricultural commodity next only to rice production (1988-89).[44] The breedable[45] cow and buffalo population is important for milk production. India has about 55 million breedable cows and 32 million buffaloes. The world milk production in 1990 was nearly 531 million tonnes (FAO, 1991) and that of India 52 million tonnes, accounting for about 10 per cent of the total World production. A comparison of milk production in individual countries reveals that India which was used to import milk has emerged as the second largest producer to milk in the world after the United States (67 million tonnes). Inspite of having a huge breedable bovine population (77 million) the total milk production in the country is only 55 million tonnes (1991). In comparison, the USA with about 10.2 million breedable milch cows, registered milk production of about 67 million tonnes in the same year.[46]

Proteins of high biological values are derived mainly from animal sources, and these are essential for growing children, expectant and nursing mothers, old and the infants, and heavy manual workers. Milk constitute the principal source of animal protein for India's population where the consumption of bovine meat is quite small and slaughter is limited.

The human population in India was nearly 844 million in 1991 while milk production was about 35 million tonnes, giving a per capita per day availability of 174 gr. as compared to the minimum nutritional requirement of 250 gr. recommended by the Indian Council of Medical Research[47] (ICMR). This clearly shows a wide gap between availability and requirement of milk. In comparison, the World human population was 5,294 million and a total milk production of 531 million tonnes yielded a per capita per day availability of 275 gr.[48] Further, a comparison of milk availability to various countries showed that in terms of per capita availability, India ranked 57th in the world, whereas in terms of milk production it raked a mighty second.

All this is due to low productivity of animal and over population (human). The low milk production in India is due to extremely low production potential of animals and lack of inadequate nutrition and health coverage. The current inadequacy in the quality of livestock, feeds and fodder and health protection facilities are the result of past neglect.[49]

A casual look at the above parameters to a layman may appear disturbing, rather frightening. But we have nothing to be ashamed of. In fact, our dairy sector has made impressive gains and we have every reason to be proud of it. Today India has the fastest growing dairy industry in the World. In this context, Verghese Kurien, Chairman of the National Dairy Development Board (NDDB), correctly put it "Dairying in India has come of age".

The gap between requirements and availability of milk and milk products can be bridged by an aggressive cattle and buffalo development programme, comprehensively organised and effectively implemented. To promote the bovine economy the government appointed several committees of agriculture and livestock experts since the beginning of this century at the national and the provincial levels. These committees have commented on the nature of the livestock problem and suggested ways of improving the productive efficiency of the livestock. All these examinations indicate tremendous potentiality for cattle development in India in the overall plans for rapid economic growth and desirable social change. If cattle and buffalo development programmes are pursued with vigour, the commodities available from these animals will in future meet not only the increased domestic demand but promote possibilities for export and import substitutes. This will greatly enhance the scope for income and employment in the rural economy.[50]

In response to Government efforts, the dairy sector of the country has witnessed change in the last two decades, since 1970. Impressive gains have been made in the country's annual milk production and productivity per animal has also increased. The per capita milk availability has gone up from 110 grams in 1973 to 174 g. in 1990. The number of dairy plants have multiplied and a large infrastructure for procurement, processing and marketing of rurally produced milk has been created. The urban milk supplies have been considerably expanded. A nation-wide net work of multi-tier milk producer cooperatives, democratic in structure and professionally managed has come into existence. The milk procurement prices paid by the cooperatives have increased. Milk producers now earn more income due to stabilization of milk prices between lean and flush seasons and creation of infrastructure of dairy cooperatives and milk collection centres for wider and interior areas. A milk Grid has been established to even out seasonal and regional imbalances in milk production. Dairy equipment manufacture has grown to such an extent that most of the industry's needs are met indigenously.[51] All these achievements could well be attributed largely to the interventions made by "Operation Flood"- the largest dairy development project of the World. All this has happened and many more changes are in stock for the future.

3.1.3 Dairying in India is a Small Man's Business

The Western-style commercial dairy farming, mainly based on food grains or lush green pastures, is an important scenario.

In India we need food grains for our teeming millions and could ill-afford a luxury to feed our cows and buffaloes on western style and standards. Further the concept of dairying in India and the world is quite different. The base of Indian dairying is a small holder (small and marginal farmer and the landless) with one or two milch animals raised on crop residues and by-products with under employed family labour - mostly female work force.[52]

There is extreme inequality in the present distribution of land in India which emphasises the basic cause of the problem of small holders. In contrast, significantly the distribution of milch animals in rural areas is less skewed as compared to land and productivity of animals kept by small farmers does not compare unfavorably with that of large farmers.[53] The information available is inadequate in respect of the distribution of boviness among the individual farm sizes and among the landles rural households for the country as a whole, although some studies do exist for individual regions. On the basis of certain regional studies, the National Commission on agriculture has estimated that 70 to 75 per cent of the households possessing milch cattle belong to the vulnerable category of small farmers, marginal farmers and landless agricultural labourers.[54] A village enumeration survey conducted by the Development Board in 1984[55] covering nearly six million households in 20,386 dairy cooperative villages spread over 108 milk sheds in the country made some interesting revelations. Nearly 60 per cent of the total rural households own milch animals generally two or three. Some 72 per cent of the families owing milch animals are landless, and small and marginal farmers. The vulnerable group of families accounted for about 61 per cent of total buffaloes and cows in the survey area.

A study by the National Council of Applied Economic Research, 1991, finds that 43 per cent of the member households of milk producer co-operative societies in Operation Flood areas have only one milch animal and almost 75 per cent of the members belong to the category of landless, marginal and small farmers. Over 60 per cent of the milk output in the Operation Flood areas comes from these households.

Although returns from these animals are low, they are still cost effective. In the absence of any alternative employment opportunities, the dairy animals, therefore, could play a much greater role in the economic life of small and marginal farmers and the land less than that of medium and large farmers who derive a greater part of their income by growing crops. Thus dairying, by and large is a small man's business.

Table 3.1
Land and Milch Animal Holdings of Rural Households

Sl. No.	*Category*	*Landless*	*Marginal farmers*	*Small farmers*	*Medium farmers*	*Large farmers*	*All*
1.	Families (Millions)	2.131 (35)	1.690 (28)	1.025 (17)	0.675 (11)	0.508 (9)	6.029 (100)
2.	Families owning milch animals (millions)	0.770 (21)	1.052 (29)	0.799 (22)	0.559 (16)	0.445 (12)	3.625 (100)
3.	Animals (Millions)	1.390 (16)	2.091 (23)	1.932 (22)	1.651 (18)	1.877 (21)	8.941 (100)
4.	Animals@ per owner (No.)	1.8	2.0	2.4	2.9	4.2	2.5

Source: NDDB Village Enumeration, 1984.A Census of Six million households in 20,386 dairy cooperative villages spread over 108 milk sheds. Definition of farmers according to holding size of irrigated land: Landless; No land; marginal farmers; Upto 1 hectare; Small farmer; 1 to 2 hectares; Medium farmers; 2 to 4 hectares; large farmer; 4 ha. or more.

@ Buffaloes and Cattle male and female of all age groups.

* Figures in parentheses are percentages to the total.

Increasing milk production is one way by which we can solve the poverty problem of marginal and small farmers or even the landless labourers. But to make this venture a worthwhile proposition, provision of a remunerative market outlet is a must. Rural poor are mostly powerless. They are illiterates, are not organised and do not have assets and sufficient skills.[56]

Since small farmers are not organised, the middle men who come between the producer and the final consumer tend to exploit them and reap the fruits of the big margin available between what the consumer pays for the final finished product and what the producer of the basic material receives.

This is where the National Dairy Development Board (NDDB) through the vision of its Chairman, V.Kurian, made the much needed interventions and successfully conceptualised, designed, organised and implemented "Operation Flood", ensuring a remunerative market outlet to milk producers round the year through the organization of Anand Pattern Milk Producer's Cooperatives and providing regular supplies of milk to urban consumers at reasonable prices.[57] The experience of "Operation Flood" reveals that technological inputs in isolation cannot increase milk production, unless there is assurance of year-round market of milk at remunerative prices.

3.1.4 Dairy is an Instrument for Drought Proofing

India is charactertised by dry land/rainfed land that constitutes about 70 per cent of arable land. These areas face great instability in crop production due to erratic and inadequate rainfall. In the face of uncertainties in the crop production due to dryland/rainfed farming, livestock production has been found to provide economic stability to the farmers. The dry land/rainfed land can sustain livestock better than crop production.

Mittal, J.P. and Shiv Prasad in their study (1990)[58] "Place of Dairy Farming in Arid Agriculture" observed that drought occurrence has less effect on dairy production. It is essential that during the drought years, while crop production falls to less than 10 per cent of the production of a favourable year, the production of milk is still over 50 per cent of that of a good year. The study concludes that dairy farming by its very nature offers, therefore, a scope for remunerative employment in arid districts of Rajasthan, Gujarat and Haryana. In fact it has been recognised as an instrument of drought proofing and arid regions in India are the home tract of best dairy breeds of the country, namely, Red Sindhi, Sahiwal, Gir, Tharparkar, Rathi, Kankrej and Haryana, well known for their milk production potential and efficiency.

R.K. Patel[59] in his study made an attempt to compare the production and productivity of bovines in different agro-climatic conditions in the country. For this purpose, different states of the country which are important from bovine production angle were grouped into six groups.

(a) low rainfall and low irrigation (Gujarat, Madhya Pradesh and Rajasthan)

(b) low rainfall and high irrigation (Haryana, Punjab).

(c) Medium rainfall and low irrigation (Karnataka, Maharastra).

(d) Medium rainfall and Medium irrigation (Andhra Pradesh, Bihar).

(e) Medium rainfall and high irrigation (Tamil Nadu, Uttar Pradesh).

(f) High rainfall and low irrigation (Kerala, Orissa and West Bengal).

The study made some interesting findings. Important conclusions drawn are as follows:

(a) The analysis reveals that low rainfall and high irrigation group has shown tremendous potential for milk production. The cattle density is the lowest in this group where the buffalo density is the highest. The productivity of both the species is also the highest in this region. The availability of feed resources is also the highest in this group. The fact that the large percentage of area under fodder crops to total cropped area shows that the milk producers are aware of the potentiality of green fodder and higher milk production. Of late milk producers in this region also going for scientific dairy farming practices. Thus this group of states has emerged as a high milk producing region. The potentiality for higher milk production can be harnessed in this region by providing better marketing infrastructure, remunerative procurement price support, transport and processing facilities and redistribution to deficient states which will enable to reduce regional imbalances.

b. Surprisingly, low rainfall and low irrigation group of states emerged as the next potential region for milk production. The density of both cattle and buffalo population is relatively lower. The availability of feed and fodder is relatively high with larger area under fodder crops and pastures and grazing lands. The productivity of bovines is also next to low rainfall and high irrigation region. These facts suggest that in absence of adequate rainfall and irrigation potentiality for crop production, the farmers have resorted to dairy farming to supplement their income.

c. High rainfall and low irrigation group of states has come out to be low milk producing region. Orissa in this group has shown least potentiality for milk production with all parameters at the lower level. On the other hand, Kerala inspite of having resource constraints has shown greater strength in increasing milk production particularly that of cattle. This is the only state where productivity of cows is better than that of buffaloes. West Bengal, on the other hand, has shown potentiality for milk yield among different buffaloes. The cattle density is the highest where as buffalo density is the lowest. Inspite of having poor feed resource base, buffaloes have shown greater productivity. Further, the growth raters in milk production in both Kerala and west bengal were high which could be due to low base level milk production.

d. In general, low irrigation group of states has shown a tendency to go for dairy farming to supplement their income. The milk production and productivity of bovines are picking up in this group of states. Dairy farming thus can form a backbone for increased employment opportunities and income generation in this group of states.

3.2 CATTLE DEVELOPMENT PROGRAMMES IN INDIA

3.2.1 Cattle Development in India Before Independence

India possess an enormous cattle and buffalo population.According to the Royal Commission on Agriculture (1928) role of cattle in India was mainly as the supplier of bullock power for the cultivation. In their (commission) opinion, the type of cow suitable for the average cultivator would be the one capable of producing a strong calf and yielding in addition 1,000 to 1,500 Lbs of milk per lactation for household use. Further, the Commission was of the view that under the conditions commonly found in villages, it was unlikely that selling of dairy produce would more remunerative to cultivators than raising of crops. While discussing the production of milk for cities, it was pointed out that owners of dairy cattle should aim at producing high yielding cows with a production level of 3000 Lbs of milk per annum and not at the level of the dual purpose animals giving 1000 to 1500 Lbs of milk. The Commission anticipated that commercial dairy farms for supplying milk to the cities were likely to resort to crossbreeding in the future.

There are a number of fine breeds of cattle available in the country that could provide good foundation stock for initiating cattle development programmes. The establishment of cattle breeding farms for cattle development thus formed an important part of the earlier activities of the Animal Husbandry Departments. In 1938-39 there were 53 cattle breeding farms which were mostly concentrated in the northern provinces.[60] Another important and major contribution during the late thirties and early forties in the field of cattle development was the laying down of description and definition of characteristics of different breeds of cattle and buffaloes by the then imperial council of Agricultural Research.

In rural areas though cattle breeding was being given some attention little progress was evident. A serious obstacle to cattle development in rural areas, was the presence of a large number of scrub bulls. Farmers were reluctant to get their young stock castered as it was feared that such practice would adversely affect the growth of male calves into good bullocks. Castration of Scrub bulls was carried out by the state veterinary departments but regular periodical castration campaigns were not properly organised. Thus lack of continuity in replacement of bulls and failure to eliminate non-discript young bulls from the areas where high quality bulls were introduced largely nullified cattle development programme.[61]

3.2.2 Cattle Development Under Five Year Plans

(a) Key Village Scheme

During the First Five Year Plan the Key Village Scheme (Started in 146 villages, 6 blocks) was the main plank for cattle development. The scheme envisaged a multifaceted approach to cattle development by giving simulations attention to better breeding, improved feeding, effective disease control measures, scientific management practices and organised marketing facilities. Artificial Insemination Programme also include as a integral part of the technical programme. The original intention of the scheme was that Key Village Centres should be established only in breeding tracts so that the pedigree bulls from the farms might be used intensively for breeding and that the progency should be distributed in other areas for extensive grading up to improve quality and production of the stock there. Under the second plan the scope and functions of the scheme were expanded and 197 new village blocks and 64 urban Artificial Insemination centres were started.

In December 1959, an committee was set up to review and evaluate the work done under the key village scheme and to make suitable recommendations for formulating the future programme. On the basis of the findings and recommendations made by the committee, establishment of centralised semen collection centres and expansion of area under key Village blocks in specific breeding tracts, inservice training of staff, subsidised rearing of calves, establishment of marketing cells to promote marketing facilities were included in the third plan. Under the fourth plan it was emphasised that all inputs for Integrated Cattle Development Programme should be provided under Key village scheme and that the scheme be implemented on the same lines as the Intensive Cattle Development projects though on small scale.

By the end of the Fourth Five Year Plan 583 Key Village blocks were functioning. During the Fifth Plan period, some of the Key village blocks were proposed to be merged with the new Integrated Cattle Development Programme Scheme(ICDPS) and with the milk production enhancement programmes of Operation Flood Projects (OFP) and additional 100 Key Village blocks would be setup in the areas which would not be brought under ICDP or Operation Flood Programme.

(b) Intensive Cattle Development Programme (ICDP)

The failure of Key Village Projects to produce desirable impact and the establishment of large number of dairy plants during second and third plans which suffered with insufficient quantities of milk led to the formulation of ICDP as a part of the Special Development Programme at the end of third plan. It was envisaged that these projects would be located in breeding tracts of indigenous breeds of cattle and buffaloes and in the milk sheds of large dairy projects with a view to enabling the dairy plants to collect and process milk upto their installed capacities. It was emphasised that all the ICDP should be linked up either with the fluid milk marketing schemes or milk product manufacturing projects. This was considered necessary as cattle improvement for milk production and marketing of milk had to function as complementary to each other. The programme was expected to achieve a breeding coverage of about 70 per cent of the cattle population of each project and an increase in milk production by about 30 per cent over a period of 5 years.[62] At the end of the fifth plan there were 113 ICDPs. The government of India extended 100 per cent central assistance for the projects during the third plan. After that these schemes are being continued as state plan schemes. In most of the states, this project did not receive sufficient allocations of funds because of which adequate provision of inputs and services could not be made.

According to the programme evaluation organisation of the Planning Commission (1970-71) the ICDPS programme received a setback even in its earlier stages of implementation when these projects were transferred to the state sector with consequently financial cuts in central assistance.

(c) Artificial Insemination

A large majority of the indigenous cattle are non-descript and are low and inefficient producers. However some well developed indigenous breeds/types of cattle exist in different parts of the country which have been evolved over generations by the professional cattle breeders. There are about 26 breeds of cattle and 7 breeds of buffaloes in the country which have been recognised and classified into milch, duel purpose and drought types.[63] However, breed characteristics have so far been laid down by the Indian Council of Agricultural Research (ICAR) in respect of only 12 breeds of cattle and 4 breeds of buffaloes.

Throughout the first half of the century, there seems to have been a general consensus on the need to improve the quality of the drought and milch cattle simultaneously. The policy of evolving better duel purpose breeds accepted in the key village scheme during the fourth plan to promote the genetic potential of the cattle for milk production and to improve the quality of the male stock.

The policy underwent a dramatic change in favour of breeding high quality milch animals by around the mid sixties. The animal husbandry experts and policy makers argued that the country may have to adopt cross-breeding of the indigenous stock with exotic bulls to achieve a quick break-through in milk production. There are of course certain advantage to be gained form a strategy of cross breeding the indigenous cattle with exotic species. The cross breed cows have a lower age at first calving, longer lactation length and shorter inter-calving interval; they also convert feed into milk more efficiently than the indigenous breeds.[64]

The shift in policy found concrete expression in the launching of the ICDP and has been further intensified in the operation flood projects. The process was given a fillip by the improvements in the artificial insemination technique-based on quick freezing of semen capable of being stored for long periods and transported to long distances which made it more possible to accelerate the pace of upgradation of the genetic potential of the stock than was possible with the conventional selective breeding techniques

Currently, India has a large net work of more than 30,000 AI Centres both in the cooperative and government sectors carrying out about 15 million inseminations, but the number of calves born are less than 15 percent of the AI carried out.[65] Because the conception rate through AI in buffaloes is much lower than cows under field conditions.

3.3 DAIRY DEVELOPMENT PROGRAMMES IN INDIA

3.3.1 Before Independence

Organised dairying commenced in the country towards the end of the 19th century, primarily for the benefit of the armed forces and their families. Efforts were also made to encourage private entrepreneurs to manufacture whole some table butter, particularly for British troops. As a result, modern dairy plants were founded mainly for manufacture of table butter at Aligarh, Bombay, Calcutta, Darjeeling, Kanpur, Poona and some other towns by Messrs Keventers in the early part of the 20th century. Messrs Polsons also started manufacturing of table butter in Bombay in 1915.

In 1916, the Board of Agriculture of the Government of India reviewed the position of dairying and recommended the appointment of an Imperial Dairy Expert to organise training programmes for the local people to acquire competence in the dairy activities and to advise the central and provincial governments on improvement of dairying and establishment of commercial dairy industry in India. In 1920 Government of India appointed the first Imperial Dairy Expert in 1923 the Imperial Institute of Animal Husbandry and Dairying was established at Bangalore to function under his control. The institute also started a two year diploma course in Dairying.

The Royal Commission on Agriculture (1928) recommended improvement of indigenous breeds of cow and buffaloes with bulls of exotic dairy breeds. It further felt that the cooperative milk supply societies could not solve the problem of urban milk supply at cheap rates so long as milk production was based on poor fodder and low producing cattle.

N.C. Wright, the Director of Hannah Dairy Research Institute, U.K. was invited by the Government of India in 1936 to study the then existing dairy situation and to recommend measures for further development of dairy in the country. One of the most important recommendations of Wright was establishment of dairy research institute of high standard in the country. In accordance with the recommendations of Wright, the Imperial Institute of Animal Husbandry and Dairying was recognised in 1941 and renamed the Imperial Dairy Institute.

The Famine Inquiry Commission (1945) emphasised inter-alia the need for developing feed and fodder supply for increasing milk production. The commission recommended a study, of the place of milch animals in the farming economy of small holders in different places and the cost of milk production. It emphasised the need for increase in the milk production and consumption in villages and the need for a milk policy for urban milk supply that should recognise the prior claims of the vulnerable groups.[66]

In 1945 the Government of India decided to take measures to safeguard supply of hygienic milk to major cities. A beginning was made in Bombay and for the first time in India, milk produced in rural areas of Kaira district was collected in bulk, pasteurised and transported by rail for distribution in Bombay.

The then Government of Bombay took a number of measures on the milk front as early as 1943 by starting a subsidised milk distribution scheme. The scheme was operated by the Bombay Municipality and the Government of Bombay met all the expenses and the subsidies. After spending over Rs. 3 crores, the subsidised milk scheme was closed down on February 28, 1947, and in its place a new subsidised distribution scheme was started. Pasteurised and bottled milk was put up for sale for the first time in India for the use of the common man on December 15, 1950 from the first large dairy setup at Aarey.[67] During this period the Kaira District Cooperative Milk producers union was formed and it started supplying pasteurised milk to Bombay from Anand 400 Km.away.

3.3.2 Dairy Development After Independence

In the first five year plan the dairy development programme was initiated in relatively small way as funds were made available only out of overall savings form other sectors. Work on dairy development was undertaken in Andhra Pradesh, Bihar, Madhya Pradesh, Orissa, Tamil Nadu and Uttar Pradesh. In 1955 the Central Dairy Research Institute transformed as the National Dairy Research Institute (NDRI) was shifted from Bangalore to Karnal. The southern regional station of the newly created National Institute was opened in Bangalore.

In the second five year plan (1956-61) dairy development programme envisaged the establishment of 36 liquid milk plants for supply of milk to large consuming centers with more than 1,00,000 population; three creameries, three milk product factories and expansion of some cattle salvage and fodder forms. The second plan included expansion of the National Dairy Research Institute and its Southern regional station at Bagalore and establishment of two more regional stations at Calcutta and Bombay to meet the requirements of trained personnel for industry as well as research.

The third five year plan (1961-66) included establishment of 55 milk supply schemes for cities and industrial township, 8 rural creameries, 6 milk production factories, 2 cheese factories, 4 cattle feed compounding factories; and completion of spill over schemes of the second plan. In 1962 the government of India constituted a Working Group to study the prospects of dairy development and animal husbandry through cooperative organisations. The Groups agreed with the proposals made in the third plan that dairy development should be attempted through cooperatives and recommended steps implementing under this policy. It also recommended that to provide coordination, technical assistance and guidance, state federation of dairy cooperatives should be organised at the state level and an All India federation might be organised to coordinate the work of the state federations. It suggested that dairies with a capacity of 20,000 literes or below and "at least 50 per cent of the milk product factories should be in the cooperative sector and the reminder in the public sector". The group gave model bye-laws and working plans, identified the capital needs for cooperatives and indicated the pattern of financial assistance and support that should be provided by Government and Banking Institutions.

The organisational setup best suited to milk production, procurement and marketing had been evolved during the first three five year plans.[68] During the mid-sixties it was clear that the dairy development programmes of the country could be best served by effectively linking up milk sheds with major urban markets. The Anand and Bombay link up provided a best example.

The National Dairy Development Board (NDDB) was set up by the Government of India in 1965. It was charged with the major objective of providing on a non-profit basis, any technical services, which implementing agencies might require, in building up their dairy projects. These services were designed to help build up rural milk producers cooperatives based on the lines of Kaira District Cooperative Milk Producers' Union Limited.

The physical targets under Fourth Plan (1969-74) envisaged setting up of 41 milk supply schemes, 11 milk products factories and 43 dairy centres. During this period "Operation Flood" was conceived and formulated by the NDDB. To execute this project the Central Government setup the Indian Dairy Corporation.

3.3.3 Operation Flood Project

The Operation Flood project was conceived and formulated by the National Dairy Development Board and executed by the Indian Dairy Corporation. This project was initiated in July 1970 is the world's biggest milk drive launched in any country. Operation Flood was launched with the overall goal of laying the foundation for a modern dairy industry in India, which would be able to meet the country's needs for milk and be capable of self sustaining growth. The precess of dairy development was to be promoted by increasing milk production and milk procurement in rural milk shed areas. Basically, the milk supply was to be increased by developing a net work of so-called "Anand Pattern" dairy co-operatives of milk producers as they have evolved in the Kaira district of Gujarat State, India since 1946.

The first phase of the operation flood progrmme (OF-I), originally scheduled for five years was ended in March 1981. The funds needed for its implementation were generated by the sale of donated stocks of butter oil and skimmed milk powder, after recombination of milk, for the benefit of India's urban population. These aid commodities, in turn, were freely obtained from the EEC's surplus stocks and donated through the World Food Programme. OF-I covered eighteen rural districts, later to be extended to twenty seven districts and involved the participation of 1.4 million rural families. The main objective of OF-I was to capture a commanding share of the metropolitan milk markets, namely, Delhi, Calcutta, Bombay and Madras. The second phase of Operation Flood (OF-II) launched in 1979, aimed at bringing much wider areas. OF-II was to link one hundred and fifty seven major towns to rural milk sheds, there by covering 155 districts and 10 million producers. OF-II was financially supported by both EEC (dairy aid commodities) and the World Bank (financial aid). In 1986 OF-III was proposed by the India government to the EEC and the World Bank to further extend and consolidate the infrastructure for milk procurement, processing and marketing established under OF-I and OF-II. OF-III is being implemented upto 1994. Major National level institutions involved in the implementation of the successive phases of this programme have been the National Dairy Development Board (NDDB) and the Indian Dairy Corporation (IDC). Recently IDC had been merged with the NDDB.

(a) Objectives of Operation Flood Project

The goal of social justice, to be brought about by organising the rural milk producers in a co-operative frame work, appears to have been a major justification for adoption of the OF programme by the Government of India. They emphasis on the improvement of economic basis of small and marginal farmers and agricultural labourers, inter-alia, can be found in the objectives of OF-I[69]

(a) To make available wholesome milk at stable and reasonable prices to the bulk of city milk consumers, including vulnerable groups, namely pre-school children, and expectant mothers with major effects on protein intake.

(b) To enable the dairy organisations involved in the project to identify and satisfy the needs of consumers and producers so that consumers' preferences can be fulfilled economically and producers can earn a large share of rupee paid by consumers for their milk.

(c) To improve productivity of dairy farming in rural areas with the long-term objective of achieving self sufficiency in milk there by bringing major increases in agricultural output and incomes with special emphasis on improvement of the income of small farmers and landless people.

(d) To remove dairy cattle from the cities where they represent a growing problem of genetic waste, social cost and public health.

(e) To establish a broad basis for accelerated development of the national industry in the project period as well as the post project period.

(b) Marketing and Processing

The procurement/processing action line of the Operation Flood programme is characterised by a simultaneous emphasis on fluid milk procurement at the village level and industrial processing at the district level. The processing activities, which traditionally have taken place largely in the rural households and villages, are to be transferred to the big, newly constructed feeder (pasteurisation/chilling) and feeder-balancing (pasteurisation and milk powder production) dairies mostly with a dairy processing capacity between 1,00,000 and 1,50,000 liters. These dairies, in turn, supply milk to the so called "mother dairies" in the metropolitan cities as well as town with more than 1,00,000 inhabitants. As the name indicates, the feeder-balancing dairies are supposed to convert flush season surplus into milk powder and butter oil for replenishing lean season shortages. In addition to skim milk powder, other dairy products, such as table butter, cheese and baby food were to pay an increasingly important part in the marketing strategy of the cooperatives.

(c) Production Enhancement

The Operation Flood Strategy involves an integrated approach towards production enhancement. Attention is given to the main aspects of dairy husbandry, such as improved feeding and breeding, fodder production, animal health cover and extension, cross breeding projects i.e., the upgrading of indigenous stocks through cross-breeding with western dairy breeds, figure prominently in the plan documents especially in the plans for the second phase of operation flood.

(d) Anand Model

Operation Flood has also been described as a large scale effort to replicate all over India the pattern of milk producers organisation as it evolved in the Kaira district of Gujarat since independence. Till the establishment of a cooperative milk marketing federation in Gujarat in 1974, the Anand pattern of milk producers organisation consisted a two-tier structure: a district union, and the affiliated village dairy cooperatives. The village societies conduct the routine business of collecting, testing and paying for the milk to the producers who supply milk to the cooperatives. Besides, the village level societies provide micro level inputs like computed cattle feed, green fodder seeds, veterinary first aid and artificial insemination services.[70]

The unions are responsible for the transport, processing and further marketing of milk and milk products. Under the two-tier system, the district unions have been managing the centralised facilities at the district level, such as the feeder - balancing plant, the cattle feed factory, the semen bank and the mobile veterinary units. An important function of the district unions has been to constantly guide, supervise and control the village level societies in accordance with the model by-laws and guidelines.[71] These by-laws constitute the legal core of what has come to be known as the Anand pattern.

Where a co-operative milk marketing federation has been established, this apex body (the third tier) co-ordinates the production planning of the unions with in a state and implements marketing programmes on behalf of the Dairy later[72] The three-tier system introduced under OF-II involved some significant deviations from the Gujarat Model. Where as in Gujarat the three-tier structure gradually evolved on the basis of a locally established cooperative movement, the OF-II plans envisaged that first federations are to be formed in each cluster milk shed, followed by unions and village societies. Also, under the new system these cluster federations would own the feeder-balancing plants and responsible for the supply of technical inputs to the member producers.[73]

This shift implies a temporary transfer of the managerial control of major capital assets form the union to the cluster federation level. At the same time, the federations would assume the executive authority for OF-II in various states. In other words, the cluster federations become the focus of the organisational responsibilities that were formally divided between district unions and state institutions.

The general meeting of village producer members elect the managing committee, which in turn elects its chairman. The general meeting of the district union comprises one representative from each of the affiliated village societies. This meeting elects the board of directors of the union. Besides elected directors and the general manager (as ex-officio member), the board comprises one nominee each form the registrar of cooperative societies, the financing agency (i.e., NDDB/DDC) the NDDB and the federation. The federation is to be governed by the elected chairman of the affiliated district unions. The federations's board also includes non-voting members like the managing director and the nominee of the district registrar, the cooperative bank, the NDDB/IDC and a technical expert.

(e) Implementing Agencies of Operation Flood

The NDDB was created in 1965 by the government of India as a registered society with the main purpose of helping to replicate cooperative milk unions on the Anand pattern. The NDDB is the "think-tank" and planning agency of the whole operation. In the implementation stage NDDB acts as the source of technical expertise and assistance in helping to build cooperative milk producers societies at the village level, preparing arrangements for veterinary inputs and extension services in connection with the setting up of Anand pattern cooperatives in different parts of India. In recent years the FAO, World Bank and other international organisations have been instrumental in promoting the NDDB as a consulating agency to supply management and technical expertise to other countries.[74]

The Indian Dairy Corporation (IDC) was set up in 1970 under the Indian companies Act of 1956 to achieve the objective of the Operation Flood project. It had an authorised capital of Rs. 10 million fully subscribed and paid by the Government of India. The Union Ministry of Agriculture was formally in control of the IDC. The IDC handled and disbursed the

Operation Flood Funds. It also imported and distributed the donated commodities within India. It has the authority to formally approve plans prepared by NDDB on behalf of the state cluster federations and unions for implementing Operation Flood within individual states. Finally, it was responsible for the management of National Milk Grid and the pooled buffer stock of skim milk powder and butter oil. In 1987, following recommendations of the Committee, the IDC was dissolved and its functions were taken over by the NDDB which henceforth was granted corporate status. From their respective dates of inception NDDB and IDC had a common Chairman.

(f) Achievements of OF-I

Operation Flood-I was originally scheduled for five years but it was extended over a period of eleven years (upto 1981), partly due to delays in implementation and partly due to delay in the delivery of commodities. According to the WFP Technical Evaluation Mission, one of the problems which the project faced was the slow start in the ability of city dairies to utilise commodities in 1970-72 due to delays in the expansion of existing dairies followed by the world crisis in dairy commodities which severely curtailed WFP's shipments to the projects.[75]

The achievements under OF-I can be assessed by relating the available data on its performance to the targets set out under various action items. The aim of the action items 1 and 2 (urban processing) was to capture a commanding share of the milk markets in the four metropolitan cities. More over the food aid commodities utilised by the city dairies in the primary stages of the project were to be progressively replaced by indigenously procured milk. Indigenous procurement of milk in four Metropolitan towns rose from 70,000 LPD (liters per day) in 1970 to 1,50,000 LPD in 1981-82.[76]

Organised dairies in four major cities obtained an average market share of 55 per cent instead of the target 70-75 per cent. 17 new feeder-balancing dairies were built during OF-I. The average capacity utilization of the feeder balancing dairies was 77 per cent in December 1980 slightly less than what IDC (1981) considered to be normal utilization level. The districts were to mange some infrasturctural facilities like cattle feed plants, semen demonstration farms. In all 12 bull mother farms, 13 frozen semen banks and 16 new cattle feed plants were established. Under OF-I 1,40,000 improved buffaloes and 37,000 crossbreed calves were reported to have been born compared to a target of 1.4 million. The production enhancement component of the programme was clearly less successful than the enlargement of marketing and processing capacity,a pattern which was to continue under OF-I.

(g) Objectives of OF-II

Where OF-I was confined to the rural hinterland milk sheds of the four metrocities, OF-II assumed a national scale by aiming to cover all major milk-sheds of India. Compared to OF-I, OF-II was planned as a much more ambitious undertaking. It envisaged a fundamental transformation of the livestock and dairy sector in India.

The objective of OF-II were:

(a) To enable to million rural milk producers' families to build a viable, self-sustaining dairy industry by mid-1985.

(b) To enable the milk producers to rear a National Milch herd of some 14 million cross-breed cows and up-graded buffaloes during the 1980's

(c) To erect a National Milk Grid Which will link the rural milk sheds to the major demand centres with urban populations totaling some 150 million.

(d) To erect the infrastructure required to support a viable national dairy industry, including a national frozen semen system; vaccine production and delivery system indigenous development of dairy processing and conservation methods(for traditional and modern dairy products) with enlarged facilities for indigenous design and manufacture of dairy equipment; provision of manpower development programmes with special emphasis on professional managerial and technical cadres for rural industries, such as dairying; and interium programmes to supply butter oil as a medium-priced cooking medium and extracted foods as the basis for infant supplementary feeding programmes, especially in integrated rural development programmes based on the Anand pattern; and erection of a Management Information systems, to provide timely information to local decision-makers responsible for development of the constituent parts of the National Milk Grid.

(e) By means of the improvements thus achieved in milk production and marketing, to enable milk and milk products to form an appropriate part of a stable, nutritionally adequate diet (currently estimated at an average per capita availability of 180 grams of milk daily) which is to be achieved for a population of 750 million during the year 1980s.[77]

The OF-II plans revealed a number of noteworthy shifts in comparison with the first phase of OF. In the first place, the stated objectives of OF-II no longer explicity mentioned the vulnerable groups in the cities and the small farmers and landless people in rural areas as specific target groups of the programme. On the other hand, the OF-II objectives envisaged supplementary infant feeding programmes in rural areas. Secondly, the removal of dairy cattle from the cities, once an important of OF-I, did not figure in the OF-II plan of action. Thirdly, and perhaps most important, the OF-II progrmme involved a shift from a two-tier structure of cooperative organisation to a three-tier structure. The three-tier structure consisted of (a) Village milk producers Cooperatives each of which were members of (b) a district cooperative milk producers' union and finally (c) a cluster federation being the federation of these unions in a cluster of five or six continuous districts. These federations were designed as the main state level implementing agencies under OF-II, and replaced the earlier established state dairy development corporations.[78] The cluster federations role in OF-II was designed to overcome the organisational constraints at the state level that were faced under OF-II, that is , the unwillingness of state dairy cooperation/departments to transfer the ownership of dairy plants to the producer's cooperative organisation. Finally, in 1986 an apex federation was established, namely, the National Cooperative Dairy Federation of India.

(h) Achievements of Operating Flood-II

Table 3.2

Operation Flood-II Sixth Plan Targets and Achievements

S. No	*Item*	*Targets 1985*	*Achievements upto Sept 1985*	*Achievement as percentage of sixth plan targets 1985*
1.	Total number of village societies	29,000	39,486	136
2.	Societies under AI	8,000	8,254	103
3.	Households covered	34,80,000	39,95,000	115
4.	Average milk procurement (MLPD)	5.53	5.60@	110
5.	Urban milk processing	4.30	5.01@	117
6.	Rural dairy Processing Capacity (MLPD)	7.60	9.50	125
7.	Number of milk sheds	-	146	-

Source: National Dairy Development Board, Operations Flood Phase-III, A proposal, Anand, Sept. 1985. Quated in martin Doornbs *et al* Dairy aid and Development Indian Operation Flood, Ibid, p. 99.

Note: MLPD =Million litres per day
A.I =Artificial insemination
@ =Average to April 1984 to March 1985.

A comparison of targets and achievements of OF-II upto September 1985 is given in the table 3.2 Compared with the Sixth Plan targets, the performance is very satisfactory.

(I) Objectives of Operation Flood-III

The objective of OF-III is to consolidate and to complete the cooperative dairy development of Operation Flood so as to achieve a strong and self-sustainable co-operative dairy sector. The OF-III document of the NDDB puts special emphasis on this consolidation effort by indicating a number of "Key Tasks". These include:

(a) Giving priority to investments in milk sheds where procurement builds up faster.

(b) Intensification of farmers organisation work in those villages where viable cooperatives can be established.

(c) Promoting self-financing animal health care and artificial insemination services, while avoiding duplication with Government agencies.

(d) Early transfer of Government-owned dairy processing facilities to the unions.

(e) Additional investments in milk marketing facilities and new product lines.

(f) Introduction of uniform accounting and management information systems.

The common denomination of these various measures appears to be an attempt to streamline the operation and to put stress on commercial efficiency.[79] The later is associated with the idea of the farmers controlling processing and marketing in contrast to the public bureaucracy.

3.4 Dairy Development and the Rural Poor in India

There are several studies giving conflicting evidences on the efficiency of dairying as an enterprise in uplifting the rural poor. There is one school of thought which feel that: The white revolution cannot help those below the poverty line to rise above it; instead the poverty line becomes a barrier, scaling off the castes without resources form the participation in the operation flood programme, precisely because the programme is designed for those with resources. More or less on a similar line Santhi Georage[80] argues that the dairy production strategy of the white revoulution is relevant only to those in rural India who have land or capital or both and also that marketed surplus and income from dairy cooperatives are directly related to asset base. This emphurism is generalised by Shah[81] who contents that the Cooperative movement has not been able to significantly modify the traditional relationship between milk production and land holding. The landless, who takes up dairying seem to face a formidable problem of cattle feed, greenfodder is not available to him because he does not have land, and the relative high prices of compounded cattle feed adds disproportionately to his cost of milk production. Again, if the purchase of milch animals is financed through a financing agency, the regular repayment of installments leaves only a small amount in his hands.

F.Van Dorstan[82] in his study also observed that, the evidence revealed a scale basis of participation in the sense that the landless contributed much less to total milk production and sales than one would expect on the basis of their share in the population. He pointed out that the small farmers, on the other hand, did proportionately benefitted from the milk sales to dairy cooperatives. He further noted that the average big and medium farmers generally enjoyed a higher dairy income than the average landless, marginal or small producers. Klaus Nyholm et al.,[83] in their study, 'Socio-Economic' Aspects of Dairy Development Report' from the Bangalore Milk Shed area concluded that "the dairy cooperatives served the interests of the big farmers and are not capable of benefiting the small peasants, has given the existing social and political situation at the local level".

At the other end of the spectrum there are a host of studies based on field level data which have found evidences to show that dairy development has helped the rural poor. An allegation which has been repeatedly made in recent past is that operation flood has been instrumental in depriving the children of poor cattle owners of the milk which they would otherwise have consumed. Bowonder et al.,[84] after under taking a detailed survey in three states found that the misconception regarding draining of milk nutrition from the rural areas and inability of cooperatives to help the poor had no empirical support. As per this study dairy development programmes have helped in stabilizing the food intake during the lean months even among the landless workers category.

Ranede *et al.*,[85] observed thus: "first it is safe to say that bulk of the milk supplies come form small and medium category suppliers. Second landless labour small and marginal farmers constitute the dominant segment in membership as well as in the supply of milk. Finally it is heartening to note that landless labourers are taking up dairy as an enterprise and as a primary occupation. It can safely conclude that the cooperative milk producers societies have succeeded not only in assisting small and marginal farmers but also the landless labourers and that they (milk Cooperatives) are needed institutions of the weaker sections of the society. They found that in Gujarat, landless and small/marginal farmers together constituted about 53.8 per cent of the milk suppliers while in mahaashtra they constituted 70.4 per cent of the total suppliers.

The Indian Institute of Public Opinion (IIPO) carried out in 1984 a survey of about 2400 producers in 17 milk sheds that were covered under operation flood - II and compared the results of the incomes generated in 1978 for which the National Dairy Development Board had comparable details. It is observed that "the Guarantee of the prices to producers has been one of the major strategies of providing incentives to farmers and agricultural labourers to develop subsidiary incomes based on an assumed sale of milk at an assured prices. Katar singh and Mukunda Das in a comparative evaluation study regarding the impact of operation flood -I at the village level in three states modestly concluded that: "Operation Flood - I did not directly seek to improve income distribution by favouring the small and marginal farmers and landless milk products in any manner. However, by providing equitable access to an assured market for milk, balanced cattle-feed animal health care and artificial insemination services to both the rich and poor milk producers, it could be expected to have some positive impact on income distribution. A field study in Maharashtra conducted by Binadir[86] found that nearly two-third of households who were members of dairy societies were from small and marginal farmers and landless-labourers. The economic plight of majority of households was considerable prior to the inception of dairy enterprise. Moreover 70 per cent of households were living below the poverty line. But while adopting the dairy business, the poverty declined by 30 per cent. Here it is argued that in many rural milk shed ares in Maharashtra, the main occupation of rural farmers is only dairying. It provides them productive and remunerative employment by which they can double their family income. This has its implication in so far as reduction in rural poverty is concerned. The Indian institute of Public Opinion (IIOP) study states, while the landless and small groups have been benefitted, it is not to be denied that the larger land lords have obtained higher income from their larger cattle and land holdings. Finally, a study in Haryana with the help of a linear programming exercise showed that live stock enterprise has got a positive effect on income and employment generation on all the sizes of farmers. Thus, the review of earlier studies shows that there is no consensus regarding the efficiency of dairying as an enterprise in uplifting the rural poor. Hence, the majority of studies formed evidence that dairy development through Operation Flood Programme has helped the poor.

3.5 Summary

Agriculture is said to be the backbone of the Indian economy. Livestock occupies second position after land and irrigation by contributing about one fourth of agricultural sectors income. The contribution of the dairy sub-sector accounted for nearly two thirds of live stock contribution; and interms of growth in accounted much higher rate (5 per cent) than agriculture.

Since beginning of this century Government of India appointed several committees of agricultural and livestock experts to promote bovine economy. All these committees indicated tremendous potentiality of cattle development for rapid economic growth and social change. On the lines of committees recommendations government introduced different schemes like key village scheme, intensive cattle development programme, promotion of artificial Insemination facilities etc.

Though organised dairying commenced in India towards the end of 19th century, sincere efforts are actually started for its promotion especially with the initiation of worlds biggest operation flood project in July 1970 by he National Dairy Development Board with the support of European Economic Community and World Food Programme and the project has implemented in three phases. In phase-I emphasis was given on the improvement of economic basis of small and marginal farmers and agriculture labourers. Phase - II envisaged a fundamental transformation of the livestock and dairy sector in India. Phase -III is launched to achieve a strong and self sustainable cooperative dairy sector in India.

In response to Government efforts in implementation of Operation Flood project the dairy sector of the country has witnessed a tremendous change especially in the last two decades. As a result the per capita milk availability has gone up from 110 grams in 1973 to 174 grams in 1990.

There are two schools of thought with regarding the efficiency of dairying as an enterprise in upliftment of the rural poor. One school of thought feels that white revolution (dairy development) cannot help those below the poverty line to raise above it instead poverty line becomes a barrier scaling of the costs without resources from the participation in the operation flood programme, precisely because the programme is designed for those with resources. At the other end of the spectrum there are a host of studies based on field data which have formed evidence to show that dairy development has helped the poor.

4

DAIRY DEVELOPMENT IN CHITTOOR DISTRICT AND (ANDHRA PRADESH)

It is always dubious to make broad generalizations about economic and social change on the basis of a few selected district studies. It is all the more risky with respect to India, where conditions differ not only from district to district but block to block and even village to village.

— *Francine R. Frankel*

4.1 Agro-Economic Features of the District

Introduction

The State of Andhra Pradesh is divided into three regions namely - Rayalaseema, Telangana and Coastal Andhra based on its geographical and economic composition. The Chittoor District is one among the four districts of drought prone Rayalaseema region.

Chittoor district is a southern most border district of Andhra Pradesh, surrounded by two other states Tamil Nadu on the east and Karnataka on the south. It lies between 12° - 37' N to 14° - 8' of North latitude and 78° - 33' to 79° - 55' of the eastern longitude. It is a combination of plains, valleys, plateaus and hills and covers an extent of 15,152 sq.km.

(a) Population

The total population of the Chittoor district as per 1991 census is 32,56,247 comprising 16,54,273 males and 16,01,974 females. The density of population works out to 215 per sq.km. This is lower than the state figure of 241. The decinnial growth rate of population in the district (1981-91) is 18.96, whereas it is 23.91 in A.P. The decinnial growth rate has decreased from 21.14 (1971-81) to 18.96 in (1981-91) the district whereas it is almost constant at the state level (23.19). As per 1991 census 80.2 per cent of the district population is living in rural areas. This figure is higher than the state average of 76.7 per cent.

(b) Occupational Pattern

Agriculture is the main occupation of the people and constitutes the key sector of the economy of the district. The bulk of its employment is generated from the agricultural sector that accounts to nearly 73 per cent of total work force, of which, agricultural labour are 35 per cent and cultivators 38 per cent according to 1990-91 census. The remaining meagre amount of work force is engaged in other two sectors viz., secondary and tertiary sectors. Even in this meagre percentage, considerable portion of people earn their livelihood by working in the occupations dependent upon agriculture like storage, processing, trade and commerce, transport of agricultural products etc., both in rural and urban areas. In the district 53 per cent of rural population are living below poverty line and the incidence of poverty among agricultural labours is 72 per cent.[87]

(c) Rainfall

In absence of any major river, the rainfall determines agricultural conditions to the appreciable extent. The district has the benefit of receiving rainfall during both the South-West and North-East monsoon periods. The season-wise distribution of rainfall for the district is presented in Table-4.1. The average rainfall is 826 mm, 44 per cent occurs during the South-west monsoon, 41 per cent in North East monsoon, 12 per cent in hot weather period and 3 per cent in

Table 4.1

Statement showing Observatory-wise Climatological Information in Chittoor District

(Averages for the period 1981-1991)

S. No.	Month	Tirupati				Arogya Varam			
		Max. temp. (C)	Min. temp. (C)	No.of rainy days	Monthly rainfall (mm)	Max. temp. (C)	Min. temp. (C)	No.of rainy days	Monthly rainfall (mm)
1.	January	29.1	15.7	1	29.4	27.1	15.3	1	8.0
2.	February	32.0	17.5	1	6.7	30.1	16.7	1	5.9
3.	March	35.4	20.6	1	8.5	33.2	19.1	1	8.7
4.	April	38.0	24.3	1	23.6	34.7	20.0	2	29.2
5.	May	38.8	25.6	4	59.8	34.7	23.5	4	57.2
6.	June	36.6	25.2	4	60.5	32.0	22.7	4	60.1
7.	July	34.4	23.9	8	89.6	30.0	21.7	6	87.5
8.	August	33.7	23.5	7	110.9	30.0	21.7	6	88.2
9.	September	33.3	23.1	8	117.7	29.8	21.2	6	108.1
10.	October	32.2	21.5	7	174.0	28.3	20.1	8	143.1
11.	November	29.3	19.4	8	181.3	26.5	17.6	5	80.7
12.	December	28.3	17.1	4	74.1	25.5	15.5	3	41.4

Source: Records of Chief Planning Officer, Chittoor.

winter period. The coefficient of variations reveal that the rainfall received during North-east monsoon period alone is some what stable besides the annual rainfall.

The temperature and rainfall of mountain plateau on the West (Arogyavaram) and the plains in the East (Tirupati) recorded are presented in Table-4.2. In Tirupati average temperature ranges from 16°c to 42°c in between January -

Table 4.2
Season-wise Distribution of Rainfall in Chittoor Dist. (mm)

S. No.	*Year*	*South-West monsoon period*	*North-east monsoon period*	*Winter Period*	*Hot Weather period*	*Total Railfall*
1.	1973-74	403	263	Nil	62	728
2.	1974-75	427	251	2	92	771
3.	1975-76	522	445	3	28	998
4.	1976-77	462	446	2	110	1020
5.	1977-78	362	500	14	90	966
6.	1978-79	416	431	42	68	957
7.	1979-80	408	424	Nil	59	891
8.	1980-81	249	300	6	111	666
9.	1981-82	497	279	Nil	52	828
10.	1982-83	296	256	Nil	68	620
11.	1983-84	616	327	115	107	1165
12.	1984-85	392	327	23	36	778
13.	1985-86	418	369	120	38	945
14.	1986-87	298	253	4	68	623
15.	1987-88	322	480	1	136	939
	Normal	364	338	27	97	826
	Mean	404.5	372.1	25.4	74.7	876.6
	Standard Deviation	102.8	86.9	42.6	33.6	165.4
	Coefficient of variation	25.4	23.4	167.6	44.9	—

Source : Season and crop Reports of Andhra Pradesh, Directorate of Economics & Statistics, Government of Andhra Pradesh, Hyderabad.

May and in Arogyavaram it ranges in between 15°c to 35° during the same period. The normal rainfall of the district is 908.1 mm which is more than other district in Rayalaseema. The average rainfall over the years is 936 mm for Tirupati and 718 mm for Arogyavaram. The average rainy days in between two stations ranges from 54 in Tirupati and 47 days in Arogyavaram.

(d) Land Utilisation

The geographical area of the district is 15, 152 sq. Km. as per Agricultural Census 1989-90, of which forests cover 30 per cent. But it is less than 33.33 per cent which is fixed as per desirable minimum in the National Policy of 1952. In this district 51 per cent of geographical area is covered by forests, barren and uncultivable land, land put to non-agricultural uses: and the corresponding figures in Rayalaseema and Andhra Pradesh are 41 and 39 respectively. Due to this the percentage of sown area to the geographical area is low in the district (32 per cent) in relation to Rayalaseema and Andhra pradesh (each 40 per cent). In the district very small cultivators, each with not more than one hectare constitute 58 per cent of cultivators in 1989-90.[88] They operate 19.3 per cent of area indicating excessive concentration of land holdings in few hands.

(e) Irrigation

The chief sources of irrigation in the district are tanks and wells. This is one of the district where under ground water resources have been exploited to a fairly large extent.

As shown in Appendix Table-1 the net area irrigated under well irrigation accounts for 74 per cent in the district where the corresponding figures are 25 and 51 per cent for A.P. and Rayalaseema. Tank irrigation accounted for 24 per cent. Canal irrigation accounted for only one per cent due to absence of any major river in the district, as against 50 per cent in Andhra Pradesh and 35.1 per cent in Rayalaseema. Area irrigated more than once is comparatively higher (31 per cent) when compared with that of Andhra Pradesh (23 per cent) and Rayalaseema (18 per cent).

(f) Cropping pattern

A large variety of crops are raised in the district both under irrigated and un-irrigated conditions. From the view point of the cropped area, groundnut is the most important crop. paddy being the staple food in the district is naturally the next important crop. Commercial crops account for 56 per cent of the total cropped area and the rest is under food crops. Among the commercial crops groundnut is the foremost, accounting 53 per cent of the total cropped area. The district ranks second in the state in groundnut production. Sugarcane is another important irrigated commercial crop accounting 5.8 per cent of total cropped area. On the whole agriculture in the district is considerably more commercialised when compared to Andhra pradesh (A.P.) (see Table Appendix-II).

(g) Livestock Economy

Live stock economy plays an important role in the economy of the state as well as in the district. In Andhra Pradesh the gross income from animal husbandry sector accounted Rs.1,589.69 crores in the year 1986-87 accounting for 23.8 per cent of gross income of agriculture and animal husbandry sectors. Of this, the gross value of milk and milk products alone was Rs.873.05 crores. The gross income was Rs.359.92 crores from poultry, 187.17 crores for meat and meat products and Rs.169.55 crores from other livestock production. However, the livestock population has decreased in between 1983 and 1987. As shown in the table appendix-III total Bovine population decreased by 3.6 per cent in AP. This decreasing tendency is much higher in chittoor district (5.1 per cent) but very much low in Rayalaseema (0.8 per cent). Bovine population has decreased comparatively at a high rate to bovine population (9.5%) in Andhra pradesh (A.P). 13.7 per cent in Rayalaseema and 11.6 per cent in the district which needs special attention. The bovine and ovine population together decreased by 8 per cent in the district followed by Rayalaseema (7.3 per cent) and A.P. (5.8 per cent). But cross breed cattle population has increased in the entire state almost uniformly (125 per cent in A.P, 129 per cent in the district).

(h) Reasons for Decrease in Livestock[89]

The general decrease in livestock was due to the prevalence of severe drought in some parts of the state on one side and heavy rains and floods in some of the districts in the state resulting finally in heavy mortality in the livestock population. The decrease in cattle was due to decrease in the category of indigenous cattle which were quite uneconomical during the drought period.

(i) Density of Livestock Population

Density of livestock population per sq.km. is an indicator to judge the concentration of livestock in different district/regions. The table Annexure-IV reveals that the concentration of livestock (bovine and ovine) is more in the district (126) than A.P. (120) and Rayalaseema (105). But the district has less buffaloes per sq.km. (15) than Rayalaseema (20) and A.P (32). This low density of buffaloes influences the density of bovine (buffaloes and cattle) population in the district. However, the density of cattle population is much higher in the district (57) than A.P (45) and Rayalaseema (36). The cross-breed population in the district presents a peculiar tendency where its density 11 per sq.km. which is absolutely much higher than Rayalaseema (3) and Andhra pradesh (1). In other words, 79 per cent of Rayalaseema or 42 per cent of A.P. cross breed cattle population is in the districts.

(j) Veterinary Services

The State Government have been undertaking a number of schemes such as provision of veterinary services, collective measures for control/treatment of diseases and also for research, training and education programmes for the development of animal husbandry. To cater the animal health, there are four types of veterinary institutions functioning in the State viz., veterinary poli-clinics, veterinary hospitals, livestock supervisory units and Rural Livestock units. As shown in the Table - Annexure V, the government is providing veterinary services at different levels to cover entire livestock population.

Appendix-V, reveals that on an average each veterinary unit covered 62.6 sq.km. in the district where as the corresponding figures are 64 in Andhra Pradesh (A.P) and 79 in Rayalaseema. Thus veterinary services are comparatively much better in the district than Andhra Pradesh and Rayalaseema.

4.2 Regional Variations in Chittoor District

(a) Geographical Area

The district consists of 66 mandals and 11252.93 sq.km. area excluding reserve forests. Since the district is heterogeneous in many respects it can be divided into three natural divisions[90] (regions).

(1) Eastern region - plains in the east
(2) Western region - Mountain plateau on the west
(3) Central region - midland areas

The central region with moderate climate consists of 12 mandals or 15.7 per cent of district's geographical area as shown in Table-4.3. The eastern region comprising 23 mandals of plains accounted for 29.7 per cent of geographical area.

Table 4.3
Geographical Area of the Three Regions

Region	*No. of Mandals*	*Area in Sq.km.*	*Percentage to the total*
Central	12	1,766.41	15.7
Eastern	23	3,344.82	29.7
Western	31	6,141.70	54.6
District	66	11,252.93	100.0

Note: *Excluding Reserve Forests.

Source : Hand Book of Statistics 1991-92, Chittoor District pp. 3&4 (Computed).

The western region consists of 31 mandals of mountain plateau accounted for 54.6 per cent of geographical area. Thus western region is the biggest region with more than half of the district geographical area followed by eastern region and central region with 29.7 and 15.7 per cent of area respectively.

(b) Population

In the district the density of population per sq.km. is 290 persons. The Table-4.4 shows that the density of population is lowest in western region (228) and highest in eastern region (448). The central region stands in between these two regions with 395 persons per sq.km. 20 per cent of district population is in urban areas and the remaining 80 per cent is in rural areas. But this tendency varies from region to region where 29 per cent of central region population is in urban areas followed by eastern region (22 per cent) and western region (11 per cent).

Table 4.4
Population Characteristics of the three Zones of Chittoor District 1991

Region/ District	*Population*			*Main Workers*		*Agricultural labourers*	
	Persons	*Female Population per '000male*	*Percentage of urban population*	*Persons*	*Female Workers per thousand male*	*Persons*	*Female labour per thousand male*
Central	6,98,241 (395)	966	28.6	2,79,170	397	99,382	766
Eastern	11,62,816 (448)	961	22.1	5,37,548	415	1,90,079	870
Western	14,00,061 (228)	967	11.3	5,84,915	573	2,00,899	964
District	32,61,118	964	19.8	14,01,633	473	4,90,360	884

Note: Figures in the parenthesis are density of population per sq.km. excluding reserve forests.

Source: Primary Census Abstract 1991, National Information Centre, Southern Region, A.P. Unit, chittoor (Computed).

In the district 43 per cent of the people are workers. Eastern region stands first with 46 per cent followed by western region (42) and Central region (40). The composition of female workers to male refers the female work participation. In the district the composition of female workers per thousand male is 473. This composition is less in central region (397) and more in western region (573). Eastern region stands in between these two regions (415).

In the district agricultural labour accounted for 35 per cent of main workers. This proportion is almost same in all the three regions. But the proportion of female agricultural labour to male varies from region to region. The over all proportion of female agricultural labour per thousand male is 884. The proportion of female agricultural labour is highest in western region (964). Thus most of the female workers are agricultural labourers.

(c) Irrigation

Irrigation constitutes an important input which influences on agricultural output. In the district as shown in Table 4.5 more than one-third (36 per cent) of gross cropped area is irrigated

Table 4.5
Region-wise Irrigation Pattern 1989-90

(in acres)

Region/ District	*Net area irrigated*	*Area irrigated more than once*	*Gross area irrigated*	*per cent of gross irrigated area to total cropped area*
Central	61,267	9,335	70,602 (26.1)	30.8
Eastern	1,81,178	39,749	2,20,926 (74.6)	77.0
Western	1,29,605	39,298	1,68,903 (32.5)	22.6
District	3,72,050	88,381	4,60,431 (51.7)	36.4

Note : Figures in the parentheses are percentages of irrigated area in Rabi to total gross irrigated area.

Source : Hand Book of Statistics 1989-90, Chittoor District pp.68-71 & 52-55.

in 1989-90 and the extent of irrigation varies from region to region. The eastern region tops with 77 per cent of gross cropped area irrigated followed by central and western regions with 31 per cent and 23 per cent respectively. Further, 52 per cent of total gross area is irrigated in Rabi season. This figure varies from 75 per cent in eastern region to 26 per cent in central region. Western region stands in between with 33 per cent.

(d) Cropping Pattern

Total cropped area accounts for 12,65,170 acres (Table 4.6). Paddy, groundnut, sugarcane, ragi, jowar and bajara are the principle crops. Groundnut ranks first with 54 per cent of total cropped area followed by paddy (19.4), sugarcane (4.9), mango (4.2), ragi (3.9), Jowar bajra (2.8) and other crops (11).

The region-wise analysis reveals that cropping pattern in all the three regions of the district is not similar. In eastern delta region only 41 per cent of crops are grown in kharif season and 59 per cent in rabi season because of north-east monsoon influence. In this eastern region paddy is the principle crop with 41 per cent of total cropped area and groundnut ranks second. This region's cropped area accounts less than one-fourth (23 per cent) of the district.

On the contrary to the eastern region agriculture in western region depends on south-west monsoon as a result 92 per cent of the area cropped is grown in Kharif season. This region with 59 per cent of district total cropped area has great influence in district's cropping system.

Though central region covers only 18 per cent of district's cropped area it has some special features. 54 per cent of total cropped area is under groundnut cultivation, sugarcane occupies the important position with 13.5 per cent, followed by mango (10.1) and paddy comes next to all the above three crops with 10 per cent. In this region 86 per cent of crops are grown in kharif season. Thus each region of the district has its own cropping pattern.

Table 4.6
Area under Principal Crops : Region wise 1989-90

(in acres)

Region/ District	Paddy	% to total cropped area	Ground nut	% to total cropped area	Ragi	% to total cropped area	Jower Bajar	% to total cropped area	Sugar-cane	% to total cropped area	Mango	% to total cropped area	Other crops	% to total cropped area	Total
Central	23.007 (58.5)	10.0	1,24,328 (96.7)	54.3	2,62.3 (49.0)	1.5	5,809 (100)	2.5	30,825	13.5	23,095	10.1	19,442	8.4	2,29,129 (85.7)
Eastern	1,18,758 (25.1)	41.4	1,11,758 (36.5)	38.9	5,463 (46.7)	1.9	13,194 (94.3)	4.6	10,850	4.6	14,332	5.0	12,666	4.4	2,87,021 (41.5)
Western	1,03,228 (71.9)	13.8	4,46,611 (99.3)	59.6	41,190 (93.6)	5.5	16,446 (99.0)	2.2	19,939	2.7	15,143	2.0	1,06,455	14.2	7,49,020 (91.8)
District	2,44,993 (48.0)	19.4	6,82,697 (88.5)	54.0	49,284 (75.5)	3.9	35,449 (97.4)	2.8	61,614	4.9	52,570	4.2	1,38,563	11.0	12,651.70 (80.3)

Note : Figures in the parenthesis are the percentage of Kharif to total respective cropped area.

Source : Hand Book of Statistics (1989.90), Ibid., pp. 52-55 (computed).

(e) Bovine Density

The composition of bovine population among region is more relevant with respect to per unit total cropped area[91]. Table 4.7 gives the stocking rates of bovine in Chittoor district, decomposed in three regions. This is natural to expect as the bovine number depends on the land area, agro-climatic conditions, availability of feed and fodder and socio-economic variables. On an average, every 100 acres of cropped area in the district sustained with 98 bovine, comprising 80 cattle and 18 buffaloes. Significant disparities are observed in the stocking rates. The Central region has the highest bovine density (136) followed by Eastern region (131) and Western region has the lowest density (41). Cross-breed cattle are mostly concentrated in central region (941) followed by eastern region (7) and western region (6).

Table 4.7
Density of Bovine Population in Chittoor Dist.
(Per 100 Areas of Cropped Area)

Region/ District	*Cattle* Crossbreed	Local	Total	*Buffalo*	*Total*
Central	94,804 (41)	1,88,514 (82)	2,83,318 (123)	29,467 (13)	3,12,785 (136)
Eastern	21,027 (7)	2,28,266 (80)	2,49,293 (87)	1,27,111 (44)	3,76,404 (131)
Western	47,876 (6)	4,38,546 (59)	4,86,422 (65)	67,141 (9)	5,53,563 (73)
District	1,63,707 (13)	8,55,326 (68)	10,19,033 (80)	2,23,719 (18)	12,42,752 (98)

Note: Figures in the parentheses are number of cows and buffaloes per hundred acres of total cropped area.

Source: 1. Hand Book of Statistics, 1993-94, Chittoor District, pp.80-91.

2. Live Stock Census, 1993, Chittoor District, Chief Planning Officer, Chittoor (Computed).

(f) Ratio of Cattle and Buffalo Population

The cattle and Buffalo population in three regions of the district and the number of buffaloes per thousand cattle heads are presented in Table 4.8. The ratio of buffaloes to thousand cattle is 220 in the district. The ratio of buffaloes to thousand heads of cattle is highest in eastern region (510), and the lowest in central region with 104 buffaloes per thousand cattle heads.

Table 4.8
Ratio of Cattle and Buffaloes Population 1987

Region/ District	*Cattle*	*Buffalo*	*Number of buffaloes per 100 cattle breeds*
Central	2,83,318	29,467	104
Eastern	2,49,293	1,27,111	510
Western	4,86,422	67,141	138
District	10,19,033	2,23,719	220

Source: Hand Book of Statistics, 1989-90, Chittoor District, pp. 87-89.

(b) Breedable Cow and Buffalo Population

Breedable cow and buffalo population is important for milk production point of view. As shown in table 4.9 the district has 3,01,367 breedable cows and 1,25,123 buffaloes. In absolute terms the western region has the maximum number of cows followed by central and eastern region. But cows per hundred acres of total cropped area is more in central region (35), followed by eastern (22) and western region (21). And the density of cross breed cows is highest in central region (30) followed by eastern region (5) and western region (4).

The position is entirely different for buffalo population. The maximum number of buffaloes are in eastern region which alone accounted for 57 per cent of the total population. In eastern region there are 29 buffaloes per hundred acres of cropped area.followed by central (8) and western regions (5). In brief, more than half of the total buffalo population is in eastern region and about two-thirds of total cross breed cows are in central region alone. Thus livestock exhibits wide regional variation along with population characteristics, irrigation climate and cropping pattern in the district.

Table 4.9
Breedable Cow and Buffalo Population 1987

Region/ District	*Cross-bread cows*	*Local cows*	*Total cows (2+3)*	*Percentage of cross-breed cows to total cows*	*Buffalo*	*Total*
1	2	3	4	5	6	7
Central	68,459 (30)	11,011 (5)	79,470 (35)	86.2	17,363 (8)	96,833 (42)
Eastern	14,652 (5)	48,755 (17)	63,407 (22)	23.1	71,022 (25)	1,34,429 (47)
Western	19,134 (4)	1,29,356 (17)	1,58,490 (21)	22.5	36,738 (5)	1,95,228 (26)
District	1,12,245	1,89,123	3,01,367 (24)	37.2	1,25,123 (10)	4,26,490 (34)

Note: Figures in the parenthesis are cows/buffaloes per hundred acres of total cropped area.

Source: 1. Hand Book of Statistics (1989-90), Chittoor District, Chief Planning Officer, Chittoor pp. 87-89 and 53-55.

2. Results of Livestock Cènsus 1987, Chittoor District, Chief Planning Officer, Chittoor, pp. 13-19.

4.3 Livestock Development Programmes in Chittoor District

In the district cattle development was taken up as early as 1958 through key Village Scheme. One centralised semen collection Centre was also established during 1962-63 to upgrade the local type of animals. At the fag end of the year 1975-76 Intensive Cattle Development Block was established under Drought Prone Area Programme bringing the 6 key village blocks under this programmes and the cross breeding work was intensified since then. As such the insemination work with exotic semen has gone up from 9,900 inseminations during 1964-65 to more than 3 lakhs with a calf crop of 85,000 improved genetic calves during the year 1989-90.

(a) Pregnancy Testing Programme

This being the best district in the state for implementing the cross breeding work,[92] Central Government has selected to implement this programme under Central Sector Scheme during the year 1987-88. The main aim of the scheme is:

(i) To identify the bulls of high genetic merit and transmitting ability for milk production through pregnancy testing.

(ii) Make available proven bulls semen for further genetic improvement in the filed.

The scheme is under implementation from 1987-88 onwards in the district. The Head office has approved 50 Artificial Insemination (AI) centres in the first phase to implement the pregnancy testing programme. These identified 50 AI centres are having a minimum of 1441 AI work to a maximum of 6301 AI work per year.

(b) Special Livestock (Production) Breeding Programme

On the recommendation of National Commission on Agriculture, Government of India has sanctioned special Livestock Production Programme as centrally sponsored scheme in five districts of AP in the year 1976-77 of which Chittoor district is one with the following main objectives:

(i) To involve the small farmers/marginal farmers and agricultural labourers in the Livestock production and to generate additional employment and income to bring them above the poverty line.

(ii) To provide higher plan of nutrition for identified and selected cross-breed heilfer calves by involving the farmers to provide optimum feeding to the growing stock from the age at 4th month to 32nd month.

Under this programme the identified beneficiaries of small, marginal farmers are given subsidy at 50 per cent and the agricultural labourers at 66 2/3 per cent towards the total cost of concentrated feed to the cross breed heifer calf. In addition to the feed subsidy the scheme also provides subsidy for Food and Mouth vaccine deforming drugs and insurance cover by 50 per cent. This subsidy is provided by State and Centre at equal ratio i.e., 25 per cent each. During the year 1989-90 an amount of Rs.40.24 lakhs was sanctioned so as to cover 2877 calves in the programme. The district stands 'First' in the State in implementation of the scheme since its inception.

(c) Animal Health Cover

Veterinary poly clinic, Chittoor, is functioning from 1st November 1984 to provide expertise treatment with special diagnostic facilities. The small animal operation theater and X-ray plant were constructed with DPAP funds. Animal Health Centre started during 1975-76 for adopting the improved diagnostic methods of diseases investigation and suggesting remedial methods for the diseases prevailing in the district through the departmental institutions. Centrally sponsored scheme on Salmonellosis and Marek's disease is also sanctioned to this district, since this district is having poultry population to a strength of more than 29.00 lakhs.

To provide animal health cover and breeding facility to interior rural areas "Animal Husbandry Mobile Inputs and Ambulatory Clinic" scheme was introduced. The Ambulatory Clinic was started during 1974-75 and Mobile project started during 1976-77. Mobile project, since started under DPAP programme was shifted to Madanapalli area during 1985-86, later another two mobile projects were started in during 1986-87 and 1989-90 at V.Kota and Piler respectively under DPAP. The Ambulatory clinic is run with department budget and mobile project under DPAP.

(d) Fodder Development

Milk is produced economically when good quality forages are fed to milch cattle and growing heifers as a greater part of the ration is grown by farmers themselves in their land holdings. Since 8 to 9 years individual farmers are encouraged to cultivate fodder crops like Naipier (NB-21 NB-18, CO-I varieties) para grass under irrigation in their land holdings.

Therefore, in order to preserve and safeguard the progeny of valuable livestock present in villages of 10 Micro water shed areas and among 31 Drought Prone Area Mandals it is proposed to introduce on large scale the fodder development activity by dry land farming and under small well irrigation conditions the perennial gross plots and establishment of pastures in Mango and Coconut orchards.

The provision of good institutional and infrastructural facilities in addition to peoples attitudes in promotion of improved livestock leads to increase the size of cross-breed cattle surprisingly (Appendix IV). The density of cross-breed cattle is 10.4 per sq.km. in the district, comparatively much higher over A.P (1.4) and Rayalaseema (3.1). This tendency of increased cross breed cattle helped to promote dairying in the district at a higher rate.

4.4 Dairy Development and Operation Flood Programme in Chittoor District

(a) Introduction

The initiation of organised milk collection from rural areas started by way of organising cooperative Milk supply unions at Chittoor/Srikalahasti/ Puttur/Kalikiri between the years 1940-45. However it is mostly the middle men that dominated the membership in the union. With the starting of Intensive Milk Supply Scheme (IMSS) in 1969 with a Dairy at Chittoor by the Government of Andhra Pradesh with a capacity of 12000 liters per day, the era of participation of milk producers began, eliminating the middle men. Under IMSS village level milk collection was organised with producers headed by their informally chosen producer representative as group leader; the individual producer quality based pricing came into practice under supervision of the Dairy officials. Dairy became the prominent rural income generating activity with the thrust of Drought Prone Area Programme/Integrated Rural Development Programme in the district from 1975-96 onwards. Organised dairy development activities were taken up by Andhra Pradesh Dairy Development Corporation in 1975. Additional processing capacities by way of Milk Chilling Centres were created, cattle breeding became an established economic practice resulting in large scale cross-breed cows generation in the milk shed area of the district.

(b) Operation Flood Programme

Though the milk shed was included as part of Operation Flood-II in 1981, the direct participation of milk producers along with Milk Production Enhancement inputs from their own source came to reality from 1982-83. Under Operation Flood-II, the approved outlay for Chittoor milk shed was Rs.486.05 lakhs against which Rs.391.87 lakhs was disbursed upto March 1987.[93] The Chittoor District Dairy Cooperative Milk Producers Union was registered on 28th March 1988 for handling of their own business by milk producers. The assets and liabilities of the Chittoor Union of Andhra Pradesh Dairy Development Cooperative Federation were transferred to the Chittoor Union with effect from 1st October 1988. Under Operation Flood-III, Rs.225 lakhs was sanctioned for expansion of Chittoor Dairy from 1,50,000 liters per day to 2,00,000 liters

Table 4.10

Cost Estimates for Expansion of Chittoor Dairy from 150 Thousand Liters Per Day (TLPD) to 200 TLPD and Powder Plant from 12 MTD to 20 MTD in Operation Flood-III

(Rs. in lakhs)

Sl. No.	*Item*	*Amount allotted*
1.	Civil workers	41.89
2.	Process equipment	49.19
3.	Powder plant	71.99
4.	Cheese equipment	20.40
5.	Service equipment	27.80
6.	Miscellaneous equipment	7.50
7.	Other (Erection, contingencies and TSF)	36.25
	Total	225.02

Source: Appraisal Report on project proposal of Chittoor District Cooperative Milk Producers union limited; NDDB, Anand, March 1990, Annexure III-3 [p. 16].

per day and powder plant from 12 metric tons daily to 20 metric tons and additional 604 lakhs for setting up a 1,50,000 liters per day unit at Renigunta (Tirupati) with evaporation facility, totaled about Rs.859 lakhs under different heads as shown in Table 4.10 and 4.11.

Table 4.11
Cost Estimates for Setting up a 150 TLPD at Renigunta with Evaporation Facility in Operation Flood-III

(Rs. in lakhs)

Sl. No.	*Item*	*Amount allotted*
1.	Civil workers	233.75
2.	Process equipment	155.29
3.	Service equipment	110.95
4.	Miscellaneous equipment	17.23
5.	Erection	25.15
6.	Contingencies	17.12
7.	TSF	28.47
8.	Pre-operative expenses	5.98
	Total	*603.94*

Source: Appraisal Report on Project Proposal of Chittoor District Cooperative Milk Producers Union Limited, NDDB, Anand, March 1990, Annexure III-4.

(c) Infrastructure for Milk Processing in Chittoor Dairy

Infrastructure for milk processing dairy units in Chittoor milk shed is presented in Table 4.12. It reveals that installed handling capacity of milk products factory Chittoor is increased from 12,000 liters per day in 1969 to 2 lakh liters per day (LLPD) by 1992-93 in response to increasing milk procurement. To convert surplus milk into milk products, cheese plant, milk powder plant, ghee plant and butter plant with the handling capacity of 3 MTD, 18 MTD, 8 MTD and 12 MTD respectively are functioning.

In order to popularise dairying in the entire district 5 milk chilling centres were started since 1977. In eastern region

Pichatur and Srikalahasti Chilling Centres started with the handling capacity of 18,000 litres per day and the same handling capacity has been continued still because the milk procurement is below their handling capacity even after 13 to 15 years (see Table 4.12). In western region installed handling capacity of Madanapalli, V.Kota and Piler Milk Chilling Centres was 31,000 litres per day which has further increased to 72,000 litres per day by 1992-93 in relation to steady increase in milk procurement. In brief, the handling capacities of milk products factory; and milk chilling centres of western region are enhanced many times; but milk chilling centres in eastern region handling capacity has not enhanced even for once.

Table 4.12
Infrastructure for Milk Processing Dairy Units in Chittoor Milk Shed/Union, 1992-93 (Region-wise)

(Litres/Metric tons per day)

Location of Milk Chilling Centre (Town)	*Year of Starting*	*Handling capacity while starting*	*Handling capacity as on 1992-93*	*Milk procured/ milk products manufacturing during 1992-93*
Chittoor - Central Region				
Milk Products Factory, Chittoor				
a) Milk Processing			2,00,000	1,92,893
b) Milk Powder Plant	1980	10 MTD	18 MTD	1,31,099
c) Cheese Plant	1980	1 MTD	3 MTD	2.9513
d) Ghee Plant	1980	6 MTD	8 MTD	1.87706
e) Butter Plant	1980	8 MTD	12 MTD	1.01077
f) Liquid Milk Plant	1969	1,20,000	1,50,000	1,16,42
Eastern Region				
a) Pichatur	1977	12,000	12,000	7,950
b) Srikalahasti	1979	6,000	6,000	5,668
Western Region				
a) Madanapalle	1979	15,000	30,000	25,701
b) V.Kota	1980	6,000	12,000	13,356
c) Piler	1985	10,000	30,000	23,726

Note: Madanapalle and Piler Milk Chilling Centres handling capacity further increased to 50,000 litres per day during 1993-94.

Source: Chittoor Dairy Cooperative Milk Producers Union Ltd., Chittoor.

(d) Milk Procurement

In Chittoor milk shed milk procurement commenced from December 1969. In 1970-71 only 9 lakh litres of milk was procured and by 1980-81 it reached to 173 lakh litres (Table 4.13). After inclusion of Chittoor milk shed under OF-II in 1981 followed by OF-III upto 1994, dairy activity in the milk shed intensified, as a result 727 lakh litres of milk were procured during 1989-90 which is more than handling capacity, 2 lakh litres a day of dairy unit. According to National Dairy Development Board (Appraisal Report 1990) in 1988-89 Chittoor Dairy unit procured 24 per cent of the total milk procured in Andhra Pradesh.

'Further to avoid excess supply of milk Dairy Union often stopped milk procurement. For example in 1991-92 dairy union has not procured milk for 10 days due to excess supply. In 1992-93, 704 lakh litres (1.93 lakh litres per day) is procured. Thus slight reduction in milk procurement from 1989-90 to 1992-93 is due to avoidance of procurement for various reasons like to right off the excess supply, machines failures etc. In view of the good milk potentiality, NDDB sanctioned Rs.6.04 crores under Operation Flood-III for additional unit at Renigunta (Tirupati) with a handling capacity of 1.5 lakh litres per day with evaporation facility to supply the surplus milk to National Milk Grid in Calcutta.

Table 4.13
Season-wise Milk Procurement Growth on Over all Milk Shed from 1969-70 to 1992-93

(in lakh litres)

Year	*Flush total (October to March)*	*Lean total (April to September)*	*Grand total (April to March)*
1969-70	0.60	2.92	3.52
1970-71	4.69	4.20	8.89
1971-72	8.27	6.89	15.11
1972-73	4.70	4.39	9.09
1973-74	7.17	6.95	14.12

(Table Contd...)

Table 4.13 (Contd...)

1974-75	10.56	9.63	20.19
1975-76	19.10	19.68	38.78
1976-77	42.52	35.10	77.62
1977-78	54.80	54.34	109.14
1978-79	78.86	77.65	156.5
1979-80	78.15	68.19	146.34
1980-81	100.38	63.37	163.75
1981-82	106.75	105.32	212.07
1982-83	195.41	144.38	339.79
1983-84	184.80	156.54	341.34
1984-85	198.66	196.09	394.75
1985-86	259.46	249.28	508.79
1986-87	309.69	257.81	567.50
1987-88	321.34	313.44	634.78
1988-89	353.78	293.99	647.77
1989-90	385.07	363.60	784.67
1990-91	371.01	366.93	737.99
1991-92	328.12	346.94	675.06
1992-93	348.58	355.98	704.56

Source: Chittoor Dairy Co-operative Milk Producers Union Ltd., Chittoor, Annual Reports.

Season-wise milk procurement trend reveals that there is no much variation from lean season to Flush season in milk procurement with some exceptions during 1980-81, 1982-83 and 1986-87. In general the seasonal fluctuations are very low. It is observed that the dominance of cross-breed cows and cropping pattern of the district is responsible for the absence of wide seasonal fluctuations.

(e) Region-wise Milk Procurement

Region-wise milk procurement analysis indicates that 60 per cent of total milk procured in the milk shed came from central region in 1992-93 followed by western region with 33 per cent; and eastern region contributed only remaining 7 per cent (see Table 4.14). Milk procurement in central region had been rapidly increasing since 1969-70 followed by western region and eastern region. Further, the growth in central and western regions is much higher during OF-II and OF-III periods than before. Eastern region also maintained a steady

Milk Procurement - Regression Analysis

Sl. No.		Linear				Log Linear			
		Constant	Regression coefficient	R^2	t-value	Constant	Regression coefficient	R^2	t-value
1.	Flush Total	-84.3224	19.3209	0.9235	16.3004*	-0.7014	2.1321	0.9568	22.0943*
2.	Lean Total	-86.2154	18.5759	0.9226	16.1881*	-0.2043	1.9032	0.9136	15.2508*
3.	Total	-170.5450	37.8974	0.9275	16.7762*	0.3465	1.9774	0.9356	17.8836*

* Significant at 1 per cent level.

Regression analysis reveals that the milk procured by the dairy during flush season and lean season has maintained statistically significant positive trend. This is confirmed by the linear model and log linear model. In the case of log linear model R^2 is higher indicating that it is more appropriate.

growth, Operation Flood Programme is more successful in central region followed by western region and eastern region.

Table 4.14
Region-wise Milk Procurement in Chittoor District (Cooperative Sector Only)

(in lakh litres)

Year	*Central region (Chittoor)*	*Eastern region (Tirupati)*	*Western region (Madanapalle)*	*Total*
1969-70	3.52	-	-	3.52
1970-71	8.89	-	-	8.89
1971-72	15.11	-	-	15.11
1972-73	9.09	-	-	9.019
73-74	14.12	-	-	14.12
1974-75	20.19	-	-	20.19
1975-76	38.78	-	-	38.78
1976-77	77.37	-	-	77.37
1977-78	104.05	5.09	-	109.14
1978-79	145.18	11.33	-	156.51
1979-80	134.92	11.42	-	146.34
1980-81	134.83	13.37	15.57	163.75
1981-82	170.78	18.42	22.87	212.0
1982-83	252.00	34.17	51.21	339.79
1983-84	253.11	30.40	57.83	341.34
1984-85	283.15	39.87	70.48	394.75
1985-86	347.63	40.28	118.8	508.74
11986-87	398.76	39.40	129.16	567.50
1987-88	452.27	51.88	130.63	634.78
1988-89	460.32	45.04	142.41	647.77
1989-90	505.94	44.46	198.16	748.67
1990-91	460.59	40.47	236.93	737.99
1991-92	412.32	33.94	228.80	675.06
1992-93	424.96	49.71	229.89	704.06
1993-94				

Note: Eastern region mandals viz., Palasamudram and Vedurukuppam border mandals of central region, supplying milk directly to Milk Products factory, Chittoor. In 1992-93 Palasamudram and Vedurukuppam supplied 1.40 and 5.25 thousand litres per day respectively.

Source: Chittor Dairy Co-operative Milk Producers Union, Chittoor.

Region-wise Milk Procurement - Regression Analysis

Sl. No.		Linear				Log Linear			
		Constant	*Regression coefficient*	R^2	*t-value*	*Constant*	*Regression coefficient*	R^2	*t-value*
1.	Central region	-94.4456	24.9819	0.9062	14.5803*	0.5577	1.8004	0.9378	18.2355*
2.	Eastern region	8.5170	2.7425	0.7503	6.4864*	0.6175	1.1288	0.7149	5.9249*
3.	Western region	9.1707	14.3467	0.5376	3.5767*	2.8045	0.9156	0.6132	4.1763*

* Significant at 1 per cent level.

Regression analysis shows that the milk procurement in the three regions of the district has maintained significant increasing trend.

(f) Market For Liquid Milk

Though milk procurement has increased tremendously in the milk shed, in absence of any major town there is no sufficient market for liquid milk. There are only two small towns namely Tirupati and Chittoor with 2 lakhs and 1.3 lakh population respectively to market the milk. Hence, marketing is a major problem to the dairy union. As shown in Table 4.15, about 4 thousand litres per day (TLPD) was sold in 1981-82 and 7 TLPD in 1992-93. In other words 3.5 per cent of procured milk in 1992-93 is sold in liquid form and remaining 96.5 per cent is forced to be convert into milk products or to market in the distance cities like Madras, Bangalore or Hyderabad. As shown in Table 4.16 Milk products Factory converted surplus milk into Skim Milk Powder, Whole Milk Powder, Ghee, Processed Cheese and Butter.

Table 4.15
Year-wise Liquid Milk Sales by Milk Product, Factory, Chittoor (1982-83 to 1992-93)

(Daily Average)

Year	*Quantity sales (in '000 litres)*
1981-82	4.32
1982-83	4.48
1983-84	4.67
1984-85	5.06
1985-86	5.52
1986-87	5.47
1987-88	5.69
1988-89	5.28
1989-90	4.70
1990-91	5.40
1991-92	5.33
1992-93	7.05

Source: Chittoor Dairy Co-operative Milk Producers Union, Chittoor.

Table 4.16
Yearly Products Manufacture at Milk Products Factory, Chittoor (1982-83 to 1992-93)

(in tonnes)

Year	Name of the produce					
	Skim milk powder	*Whole milk powder*	*Ghee*	*Infant milk food*	*Processed cheese*	*Butter*
1982-83	1,704.70	107.65	1,029.00	215.22	155.90	290.52
1983-84	1,854.00	43.10	973.82	27.50	209.90	297.12
1984-85	1,718.20	835.20	1,304.18	-	144.39	157.22
1985-86	1,742.14	487.60	1,500.58	-	197.30	-
1986-87	1,084.80	194.77	1,060.56	-	128.97	17.08
1987-88	2,559.68	1,319.45	2,383.11	-	261.62	164.94
1988-89	2,360.93	5,560.03	1,742.18	-	242.38	926.98
1989-90	2,369.00	553.50	1,878.20	-	246.10	2,239.9
1990-91	1,455.00	152.20	1,126.34	-	307.90	1,398.9
1991-92	473.40	49.30	1,287.39	-	286.70	1,315.1
1992-93	1,310.99	-	1,877.06	-	295.13	2,243.04
1993-94	1,198.56	106.67	1,690.26	-	426.57	2,010.77

(g) Region-wise Coverage of Milk Cooperatives

Organised dairy industry on cooperative lines has been avowed policy of the government. Because of their economic advantages, democratic character and social purpose, cooperative organisations are considered as prelude for all round development of dairy industry. In the opinion of V. Kurien, the Chief Architect of 'Anand Model' 'only one institutional structure has proven effective in getting dairy industry done; that is unified organisation of producers which is responsible for procuring and marketing of members milk, owned and controlled by milk producers and therefore responsive to producers need.[94] The Fourth Dairy Industry conference held at Bangalore in 1978, considered Cooperative

Products of Milk - Regression Analysis

Sl. No.		Linear				Log Linear			
		Constant	*Regression coefficient*	R^2	*t-value*	*Constant*	*Regression coefficient*	R^2	*t-value*
1.	Skim milk	2037.845	-59.2660	0.1266	1.2038	7.6401	-0.1861	0.0944	1.0219
2.	Ghee	1141.671	53.2387	0.1955	1.5589	6.9086	0.2152	0.3233	2.1848
3.	Cheese	114.0468	19.6704	0.7244	5.1275*	5.0517	0.4078	0.2466	1.8095

Significant at 1 per cent level.

The production of skim milk has down ward trend but not statistically significant. The ghee production has positive trend but not statistically significant. However, the cheese production has maintained statistically significant positive trend.

has the basic tenant of Indian Dairy Industry and it felt that "A Cooperative structure is the sheet anchor of Indias' dairy development because the resource of our farmers are circumscribed and milk production is consequently small and scattered.[95]

In view of this Dairy Cooperatives are introduced to serve as the vital instrument in current dairy development programmes and indeed payment on the basis of quality in explicitly mentioned as a fundamental component of 'Anand Pattern' dairy cooperative organisation.

The dairy cooperative movement was started in the district with the initiation of operation flood programme from 1982-83. Table (4.17) reveals that there are 1489 inhabited villages with 5,54,203 rural households in the district of which 12 per cent are members in 889 dairy cooperatives during 1992-93, and this coverage varies from region to region. Further it is observed that 64 per cent of total milk cooperatives of the district are concentrated in central region alone which accounted only 15.7 per cent of district's geographical area and coverage 39 per cent of households of the region. The western region with 54.6 per cent of total milk cooperatives and covered 5.3 per cent of households followed by eastern region (29.7 per cent of district's geographical area) with 14 per cent of total milk cooperatives covered only 4.4 per cent of rural households.

Table 4.17
Region-wise Concentration of Dairy Cooperatives and Their Coverage in Chittoor District (Rural)

Sl. No.	*Item region*	*Central region*	*Eastern region*	*Western*	*District*
1.	Inhabited villages (No)[1]	283	589	617	1,489
2.	Dairy Cooperatives (No)[2]	568	127	194	889
3.	Inhibited[3] rural Households (No.)	1,14,101	1,87,897	2,52,205	5,54,203

(Table Contd...)

Table 4.17 (Contd...)

4. Dairy Cooperatives[4] members	44,555 (39)	8,343 (4.4)	13,336 (5.3)	66,234 (12)

Note : In Eastern region, the four adjacent mandals of central region Kammapalli, Vedurukuppam, SR Puram and Palasamudram accounts for 61 per cent of dairy cooperatives of eastern region.

Source: 1. Hand Book of Statistics, 1993-94, Chittoor District, Chittor, pp. 4-5.

2 & 4 : Chittoor Dairy Cooperative Milk Producers Union, Cooperative Societies - Mandal Wise as on 30-12-1992 (General Manager), Table 18.6.

: NIC (SR) AP Unit, 1991, Population Census Abstract, Chittoor District, Chittoor.

Thus, the milk cooperatives which are said to be the basic institutional frame work of operation flood programme are concentrated mostly in central region where the density of cross-breed cows are more with compared to other two regions of the district. In brief, Chittoor Milk shed procured more than half of the total milk from central region, one-third from western region and remaining milk from eastern region. Though there are regional variations in milk procurement, in total Chittoor district is congenial for dairy. Dairy in Chittoor district has grown on sound lines. Milk procurement of the dairy have maintained positively significant trend.

4.5 Summary

The Chittoor district is a combination of plains, valleys, plateaus and hills and 80 per cent of its population is living in rural areas. In the district 32 per cent of geographical area is left for cultivation. Tanks and wells constitute the chief source of irrigation. Agriculture in the district is more commercial when compared to A.P.

The district has been divided into three natural divisions, namely central, eastern and western regions and each region has its own special features with regard to population characteristics, irrigation, cropping pattern and livestock holdings. Live stock development programmes started in the district since 1958 and then district obtained the credit as the best district in the State for implementing the cross-breeding work. Further, Government sanctioned special programmes to promote the quality of live-stock.

Dairy development activity actually started in the district in 1969 with the start of a dairy unit at Chittoor. In 1975 dairy development activities are taken up by Andhra Pradesh Dairy Development Board. After that dairy became the prominent income generating activity in the district with the thrust of DPAP/ IRDP Programmes. To promote dairy industry in the district Operation Flood programme has been implemented since 1981-82. Under this programme Chittoor Dairy received impetus for rapid development.

5

POVERTY DIMENSIONS OF AGRICULTURAL LABOURERS IN CHITTOOR DISTRICT

Poverty is a multidimensional phenomenon and thus poverty policy cannot be narrow in range, limited in emphasis or simple in solution. Indeed, the diverse facets of poverty may require seemingly inconsistent strategies.

—Poverty Eradication Foundation (U.S.A)

This chapter is divided into three sections. Section-I deals with the socio-economic conditions of sample agricultural labour households. Section-II is devoted to analyse income and employment generation in dairying and Section-III is devoted to analyse the poverty dimensions of the sample agricultural labour households.

Section - I : Socio-Economic Conditions

In an evaluation study of the dairy development through operation flood programme for agricultural labourers, it is essential to have knowledge about the socio-economic background—the caste composition, age and sex composition, literacy status, occupational structure, operational holdings and working status of the households which provide basic information and facilitate proper understanding of the results of the study.

5.1 Distribution of Sample Households

The study covers 226 sample agricultural labour households in three regions - central, eastern and western - of Chittoor district. The study includes both members of milk cooperatives and non-members in the respective villages.

Table 5.1 presents the region - wise distribution of sample households

Table 5.1
Region-wise/Category-wise Distribution of Sample Households

Region	*Dairy cooperative*		
	Members	*Non-members*	*Total*
Central	76	28	104
Eastern	12	50	62
Western	10	50	60
All regions	98	128	226

The table reveals that of all the 226 sample households 46 per cent households belong to central region, 27.4 per cent to eastern region and 26.6 per cent to western region. Out of 226 sample households 98 households are milk cooperative members and 128 are non-members. Region-wise breakup indicates that 73 per cent of the central regain, 19.4 per cent of the eastern region and 16.6 per cent of the western region households are milk cooperative members. The table further reveals that 77.6 per cent of total milk cooperative members belong to central region and remaining 22.4 per cent members to other two regions. In other words, the proportion of cooperative members to total sample households is higher in central region and much lower in other two regions of the district.

5.2 Caste Composition

Social inequality in Indian society is one of the most widely commented issues by the social scientists. The lower caste groups encounter several social disabilities which hamper their progress. Hence the rationale extending constitutional protection to scheduled castes, scheduled tribes and backward communities are also receiving several safe guards and preferential treatment by state governments. Caste system though gradually breaking down with the spread of education, awareness and learning, determines to a considerable extent the pre-occupations of the rural population. It envisages easily to identify the socially and economically weaker sections.

Since caste and socio-economic conditions in the villages are inter-related, agricultural labourers, who constitute the poorest section of the rural hierarchy, mostly belong to the socially and economically backward classes. It is observed from the Table 5.2, that out of 226 sample households 69 per cent belong to scheduled caste and scheduled tribes, 22 per cent to backward communities and 9 per cent to other castes. In brief 91 per cent of total households belong to socially backward classes. This tendency holds good in all regions with slight variation.

Table 5.2
Caste Composition of Sample Households

Category	*Central*	*Eastern*	*Western*	*Total*
Scheduled castes and Scheduled Tribes	72	45	40	157
Backward Castes	24	12	13	49
Other Castes	8	5	7	20
Total	*104*	*62*	*60*	*226*

5.3 Age and Sex Composition

Age and sex composition of the population in the household will have influence in shaping the economic activities and hence income of the household. Table 5.3 provides the details regarding the age and sex composition of the population in the sample households.

Table 5.3
Age and Sex Composition of Sample Households Population

Age group	*Central Region*		*Eastern Region*		*Western Region*		*Total*	
	Male	*Female*	*Male*	*Female*	*Male*	*Female*	*Male*	*Female*
0-14	93	90	43	39	55	52	191	181
15-60	149	143	82	81	84	82	315	306
61 and Above	7	8	4	6	9	7	20	21
Total	249	241	129	126	148	141	526	508

The table shows that the total population of the sample households is 1034 persons comprising 526 males and 508 females. Persons below 15 years are considered to be dependents who account for 36 per cent and the persons who have crossed 60 years of age are considered to be inactive persons accounting 4 per cent of the population. Further, it is observed that 60 per cent of the population are between 15 to 59 years constituting the economically active population. This table also shows that dependency ratio is comparatively more. This percentage of dependents to total population further vary from region to region. In western region 42 per cent, eastern region 40 per cent are dependents whereas in eastern region the dependents are 36 per cent.

5.4 Literacy Status

Education, formal or informal enhances awareness for a better life and generates positive impulses for socio economic advancement. It controls the attitudes, opinions and behaviour of the people and influences the economic destiny of the family. Although there has been a quantitative expansion in education it is not evenly distributed between rural and urban segments and between the different strata of the society.

It is noted from Table 5.4 that among 1034 persons as much as 62.1 per cent are illiterates. The persons having primary education constitute 20.6 per cent and those who have secondary education constitute 13.4 per cent. Persons who have higher education are only 3.9 per cent of the population in the sample households. The literacy rate varies from gender to gender and from region to region. For example among 508 females of the total population 68.3 per cent are illiterates where it is only 56 per cent in case of male population. The table further reveals that in general literacy rate is lower in western region (34 per cent) followed by central region (37 per cent) and higher in eastern region (53.5 per cent).

Table 5.4
Literacy Status of the Sample Population

Age group	*Central Region*		*Eastern Region*		*Western Region*		*Total*	
	Male	*Female*	*Male*	*Female*	*Male*	*Female*	*Male*	*Female*
Illiterates	139	168	66	78	90	101	295	347
Primary Level	61	40	31	21	37	24	129	85
Secondary Level	40	25	25	21	15	13	80	59
Higher Education	9	8	7	6	6	3	22	17
Total	249	241	129	126	148	141	526	508

5.5 Working Status

Population Census of India 1981 categorised the population based on their working status into three categories viz. main workers/ marginal workers and non workers. Accordingly, main workers are those who have worked or engaged in economically productive activity for a major part of the year or more than six months during the reference year. Marginal workers are those who have worked less than six months during the reference year and non - workers are those who have not worked in any productive activity at any time during the reference year. Based on this criteria the population in the sample households has been classified into main workers, marginal workers and non- workers. Table 5.5 shows the working status of the population in the sample households.

The table reveals that of all the 1034 persons of the sample households 47 per cent are main worker's 13 per cent are marginal workers and 40 per cent are non-workers. Among regions, main workers are more in eastern region (50.5 per cent) followed by central (48 per cent) and western regions (42.6 per cent). In dry track of western region, where irrigation as well as rainfall is very much less, 22.5 per cent of population are marginal workers due to lack of employment opportunities for the major part of the year. In eastern and central regions marginal workers constitutes 10 and 8.4 per cent of the sample population. But non-workers are more in central region (44 per cent) followed by eastern (40 per cent) and western regions (35 per cent).

5.6 Size of the Sample Households

The size of poor household is generally larger than that of rich households. Due to economic compulsions children are not sent to school, they are sent for work to supplement the meager earnings of the households or they keep in the house to look after the younger children so as to facilitate their mothers to go for work. Thus the children tend to join the ranks of traditional and unskilled pursuits reinforcing the vicious circle of poverty. 'Isolation paradox' contributes to

Table 5.5
Working Status of the Sample Population

Age group	*Central Region* *Male*	*Female*	*Eastern Region* *Male*	*Female*	*Western Region* *Male*	*Female*	*Total* *Male*	*Female*
Workers								
Main	123	112	68	61	65	58	256	231
Marginal	23	18	14	11	31	34	68	63
Non-workers	103	111	47	54	52	49	202	214
Total	**249**	**241**	**129**	**126**	**148**	**141**	**526**	**508**

the large size of the family resulting in wide spread disguised and sometimes open unemployment of varying magnitudes. The family planning on the part of the poor households is the key for success of development planning in the third world[96]. But this seems to be highly complex problem with no miracle solution and therefore possess a big challenge to the planners.

Table 5.6 presents size distribution of the sample households.

Table 5.6
Size of the Sample Households

Family	*Central*	*Eastern*	*Western*	*All regions*
0-2	7	5	3	15
3-4	47	32	27	106
5-6	41	23	22	86
7 & above	9	2	8	19
Total	104	62	60	226
Average size of the households	4.7	4.1	4.8	4.6

The table indicates that 53 per cent of total sample households have 4 members and less and remaining sample households have more than 4 members. The average size of the total households is 4.6 members. From the table it is observed that average size of the households is small in eastern region (4.1) and big in western region (4.8), which is comparatively backward.

5.7 Operational Land Holdings

Knowledge of operational holding of the sample households is very much significant and relevant for the study because agricultural income is directly related to the size of operational holdings. Operational land holdings of the sample households are presented in Table 5.7.

It is evident from the table 5.7 that of the total 226 sample households, 146 households i.e., 65 per cent are operating 130 acres of land of which 36 per cent of land is irrigated and 64 per cent of land is unirrigated. The average size of operational holding is 89 cents. Only 14 per cent of net cropped area is irrigated more than once. The table further indicates that 67 per cent of net operated land is irrigated in eastern region followed by central region with 45 per cent. In western region only 16.7 per cent of net operated land is irrigated. Average size of land holding is larger in western rainfed region (1.52 acres) and smaller in central and eastern regions, 66 per cent and 64 per cent respectively. In brief, size of operational holdings are smaller in irrigated belts and larger in less irrigated regions.

Table 5.7
Size of Operational Holdings of the Sample Households

(in acres)

Region	*Land operated households*	*Net operated area*	*Area irrigated*	*Area unirrigated*	*Area irrigated more than once*	*Gross operated area*
Central	74	49.14	22.22	32.34	9.40	63.96
Eastern	33	21.20	14.20	7.00	6.85	28.05
Western	39	59.44	9.94	49.50	1.76	61.20
All regions	146	129.78	46.36	88.84	18.01	153.21

5.8 Cropping Pattern

Cropping pattern is governed by agro-climate conditions, type of irrigation, size of land holding and nature of enterpreneuership. The cropping pattern of this sample households in three regions is presented in Table 5.8.

Table 5.8
Cropping Pattern of the Sample Households (in acres)

Crop	*Central region*	*Eastern region*	*Western region*	*Total*
Paddy	18.06	16.46	5.49	40.00
Groundnut	31.89	9.29	34.45	75.60

(Table Contd...)

Table 5.8 (Contd...)

Sugarcane	11.27	1.20	5.10	17.60
Ragi and other crops	2.74	1.10	16.16	20.00
Total	**63.96**	**28.05**	**61.20**	**153.20**

It is observed from the table that out of 153 acres of gross cropped area of the total sample households about 50 per cent is used for groundnut; 26 per cent for paddy, 11.5 per cent for sugarcane and remaining 13 per cent for other crops like ragi, jowar, chillies etc., There is much diversity in cropping pattern from region to region due to diversity in agro-climatic conditions, irrigation facilities etc. In central region about half of the gross cropped area (48.5 per cent) is used for groundnut mostly as dry crop followed by paddy (28 per cent) and sugar cane (17.6 per cent). In eastern region paddy is cultivated in 57 per cent of gross cropped area groundnut mostly as irrigated crop (33 per cent) and sugarcane 4.3 per cent. In western region groundnut is grown as dry crop in 56 per cent of gross cropped area followed by paddy (9 per cent) and sugarcane (8.3 per cent). In western region ragi is mainly grown as dry crop whereas in eastern and central regions it is grown as irrigated crop alone.

5.9 Sheep and Goat

In rural areas sheep and goat constitute an important livestock to generate regular income and employment in addition to their uncertain wage and land incomes. In villages sheep and goat are treated comparatively a liquid asset to meet the emergency financial needs of the family. In other words, households can sell them within a short notice than even cows and buffaloes. The particulars of sheep and goat assets of the sample households are furnished in table 5.9.

Table 5.9
Sheep, Goat Holdings of the Sample Households

Region	*No. of House-holds with sheep, goat*	*Sheep, Goat (Number)*	*Average value of sheep,goat per household*
Central	20	262	11,300
Eastern	7	120	12,714
Western	16	292	9,466
All regions	43	674	10,848

From Table 5.9, it is observed that of the 226 total sample households 19 per cent households are possessing sheep/goat worth Rs.10,848 per household. The proportion of households with sheep/goat to total households differ from region to region. In western region more than one-fourth of households, in central region about one fifth of households and in eastern region only one eighth of households are holding sheep/goat. In other words in hill plateau region (western) majority of agricultural labour households are substituting their income through sheep/goat rearing than other two regions.

5.10 Bullocks

In rural areas traditionally bullocks are used for ploughing and transporting agricultural produce. On the eve of mechanisation of agriculture, tractors have been substituted for these purposes. Since size of operational holdings are small in many villages on one hand and economic backwardness of the farmers on the other still bullocks are used in some areas for ploughing and transportation. Agriculture labourers hold bullocks to till their own/ leased-in land and to earn additional income and employment through hiring the bullocks. So bullocks also generate additional income and employment to the agricultural labourers. Bullocks owned by sample households are presented in table 5.10.

Table 5.10
Bullocks Owned by Sample Households

Region	*Households with bullocks (Owned)*	*No.of bullocks*	*Average value per bullock pair (in rupees)*
Central	12	24	4,900
Easter	27	54	3,940
Western	22	44	3,400
All regions	**61**	**122**	**3,959**

Table 5.10 reveals that 61 households holding bullocks worth Rs.3959 per pair. In eastern region with assured irrigation facilities regular employment is available for bullocks. In western region drought animals are numerically large and cost less. To earn subsidiary income these drought animals are used for ploughing in rainy seasons. In central region since dairying is more profitable, agriculture labourers naturally prefer milch animals to bullocks. Hence 44 per cent, 37 per cent and 12 per cent of households in eastern, western and central regions respectively owned bullocks.

5.11 Agricultural Wage Earnings

The employment pattern of agricultural labourers depends on various factors like size of land holdings, supply and demand for labour, rainfall, irrigation, cropping pattern, scale of mechanisation, use of high yielding varieties etc. For example if size of land holdings are small, farm operations are done by family labour and the demand for hired labour is limited. The demand for labour varies from crop to crop. For example demand for female labour is low when compared to male in extensive sugarcane cultivated area. The agricultural activities like ploughing, plantation, crop irrigation, sugarcane cutting and jaggery making operations mostly need male labour. But in extensive rice growing areas the demand for female labour is higher than male labour. High yielding varieties cultivation with assured irrigation is assumed to have increased employment potential since it requires regular application of water, fertilizer, pesticides, etc.

Similarly agricultural wages are influenced by several socio-economic factors like supply and demand for labour, seasonal conditions, age and sex composition of labour, bargaining strength of labour, local traditions,fertility of land, types of operation, labour skills,cropping pattern etc. Further agricultural work participation rate is influenced by various factors like wage rate, climate, nature of work, employment opportunities in non-agricultural activities where wage rate is high like .construction etc. But all these factors differ from region to region and even from village to village. Table 5.11 presents agricultural wage earnings of the sample households in three regions of the district.

Table 5.11 reveals that there are 310 male and 272 female and 38 child labourers working for wages. Male labourers are working for 155 days, female labourers 150 days and children 84 days per year and earnings on an average for these three categories are: Rs.2846, Rs.2101 and Rs.976 respectively. Sample households have 61 ploughs through which they secured wage employment in an average 110 days per annum and earned Rs.1490 per plough as wage for human labour.

Region wise analysis reveals that average working days for male is higher in central region (161 days) followed by eastern delta region (158 days) and rainfed western region (143 days). In contrast to male labour, female labourers' working days are 152 in western dry tract and 149 in central and eastern regions.

Wage rates of male are much higher in eastern region (Rs-21) lower in western region (Rs.16). Central region stands in between these two regions with Rs.18. Like-wise annual wage earnings of both male and female labourers are relatively higher in eastern region followed by central and western regions as shown in table 5.11. In brief, agricultural wage income per worker is more in delta (eastern)region and less in western region. The wage earnings in central region are less than eastern region and more than western region.

Table 5.11
Agricultural Wage Earnings of the Sample Households

Region	Agricultural Laboruers (No.)				Annual Average Working Days				Average Wage Rate				Annual Average Wage Earnings			
	M	F	C	P	M	F	C	P	M	F	C	P[1]	M	F	C	P[1]
Central	146	114	18	12	160.80	149.03	73.33	108.00	17.85	13.58	12.56	15.00	2869.97	2023.42	921.11	1620.00
Eastern	86	79	7	27	157.73	149.62	100.00	121.11	21.10	16.10	12.43	16.54	3324.41	2401.90	1242.86	1560.00
Western	78	79	13	22	142.50	151.71	90.77	96.14	15.97	12.61	10.00	13.87	2275.32	1912.28	907.70	1332.96
Allregions	310	272	38	61	155.33	150.00	84.21	109.52	18.32	14.00	11.60	13.60	2849.10	2101.07	975.80	1490.00

Note : M = Male ; F = Female ; C = Children; P = Ploughs.

1. Wage for human labour.

Table 5.12
Average Hours of Work for Agricultural Operations (Excluding break for rest)

Sl. No.	Category	Central region	Eastern region	Western region	All regions
1.	Ploughing	5.75	5.00	6.50	5.90
2.	Sowing	8.50	6.50	9.25	8.40
3.	Transplantation	7.25	5.70	8.50	7.30
4.	Weeding	8.50	6.20	9.30	8.30
5.	Harvesting	7.50	5.70	8.50	7.40
6.	Sugarcane cutting & Jaggery operation	9.20	6.00	9.80	8.80
7.	Other operations	8.00	6.00	9.00	7.90

In the district agricultural operations are mostly performed by manual labour in absence of mechanisation. Degree of mechanisation depends on size of holdings, irrigation facilities, cropping pattern and economic status of land owner and technological advancement. In the study area since size of the land holdings are very small and irrigation facilities are low, the degree of mechanisation is very limited. In few cases tractors are used for ploughing and sugar cane crushers operated by electrical power are commonly used in the process of jaggery preparation. Except these two, remaining operations are performed by manual labour.

Hours of work for different agricultural operations is not uniform. It depends on nature of work, season,demand and supply of labour in the village.

For example land is ploughed normally forenoon only, where as sugarcane cutting and jaggery preparation is a continuous process of the day even with out break. Transplantation and harvesting are time bound and seasonal activities and more labour is required at once for all farmers in the village when the demand for labour is maximum. During this period workers are made to work everyday by offering additional incentives. Working hours for transplantation and harvesting are comparatively less.Sowing is also a time bound programme but it does not require as much labour as for transplantation and harvesting- The above table presents the average hours of work for agricultural operations in the study area.

Further the table reveals that in the study area average working hours are minimum (6 hours) for ploughing and maximum (8.8 hours) for sugarcane cutting and jaggery operations. Hours of work for transplantation and harvesting are 7.3 and 7.4 respectively. For sowing and harvesting the working hours are 8.4 and 8.3.

The table further indicates that working hours vary widely among three regions. In agriculturally advanced eastern region working hours of workers in all agricultural operations is lowest but highest in rainfed western region.

Section-II : Income and Employment Generation in Dairying

Cattle rearing is an age old activity in rural areas. Most of the rural poor keep one or another type of livestock and are familiar to cattle keeping. This also suited their skills, knowledge and experience. Dairy cattle keeps the labourer busy through out the year by providing a steady and stable income and it also provides gainful employment to the educated as well as uneducated persons including female and children. In addition, adverse effects of natural calamities are less in dairying. The rural poor who may not be able to derive the benefit of agricultural programmes can look to dairy as a profitable subsidiary occupation. Since dairying is labour intensive it helps the poor, who have extra man power, to generate additional income.

Proper marketing of the produce is essential for any economic activity. In dairy development programme sale of milk at remunerative prices to the beneficiaries is crucial determinant of the success. Regular payment for milk sale is important because small milk producers mostly depend on the income from milk sale for feeding and management of dairy cattle. Anand pattern primary milk producers unions(milk cooperatives) are best suited for this purpose in many respects and assure market for the milk production, input services, production enhancement programmes etc.

As per the by-laws of Milk Cooperatives genuine milk producers owing milch animals and who have agreed to sell their milk through the cooperative milk society are eligible to become members of dairy cooperatives. Genuine milk producers who supplied 90 litres of milk or supplied milk for 90 days regularly are eligible to become members of the milk society with payment of Rs.11 as membership fee,according to amended by-laws of Chittoor Dairy Union. To obtain attractive benefits by become members almost all milk producers have joined as members. Due to liberalised entry policy (by-laws) of milk cooperatives all dairy animal owned agricultural labour households have joined as the members of the milk cooperatives. The Table 5.13 presents category-wise milch animal holdings of the sample households and their average values.

5.13 Category Wise Milch Animal Holdings

Table 5.13 reveals that out of 98 total member households 17.4 per cent possessed local cows, 71.4 per cent owned cross breed cows and remaining 11.2 per cent of households have local buffaloes. Of the total 159 dairy animals 50 per cent are cross-breed cows followed by local cows and buffaloes (25 per cent each). The average value of local cow is Rs.2239, cross-breed cow is Rs.3736, buffalo is Rs.1531 and average value of all the milch animals is Rs.2805. The value of milch animals vary from region to region depending on quality of animal and their demand and supply in the region. From the table it is observed that in central region 79 per cent of households own cross-breed cows followed by western region (60 per cent) and eastern region (33 per cent). Similarly in eastern region 50 percent of households are holding buffaloes followed by western region (10 per cent) and central region (5.3 per cent).

The composition of local cows, cross-breed cows and buffaloes differs from region to region. In central region cross-breed animals are more numerous (63 per cent)than local cows and buffaloes. In eastern region buffaloes represent 69 per cent of total milch animals. But in western region local cows accounted for 41 per cent followed by cross-breed cows (36 per cent) and buffaloes (23 per cent).

Table 5.13
Category - wise Milch Animals Owned Households (Member Households) and their Livestock Assets

(in Rs)

Category	Central			Eastern			Western			All regions		
	No.of households	*Total holdings*	*Average value*	*No.of households*	*Total holdings*	*Average value*	*No.of households*	*Total holdings*	*Average value*	*No.of households*	*Total holdings*	*Average value*
Local cows	12	26	2285	2	5	1750	3	9	2128	17	40	2238.77
Cross-breed cows	60	68	3708	4	4	4200	6	8	3743	70	80	3736.10
Buffaloes	4	14	1650	6	20	1450	1	5	1522	11	39	15.31
Total	76	108	3098.65	12	29	1881	10	22	2577.50	98	159	2804.50

Note: Live stock value in 1992 year prices.

5.14 Mode of Acquisition of Milch Animals

In rural areas livestock is acquired through different ways namely through home breed, purchased with self/ government/private financial assistance, gifts from relatives or land lords and through leasing from others. The acquisition of different types of livestock in a region is influenced by geographical conditions, climate, economic status, source of finance, profitability and government encouragement. Table 5.14 presents the mode of acquisition of milch animals by the member households.

As per table 51 per cent of total milchanimals are born at home, 16 per cent purchased with self-finance, 19 per cent purchased with government financial assistance under Integrated Rural Development Programme and Drought Prone Area Programme and the remaining 14 per cent are taken for lease from others.

Category wise analysis shows that only 39 per cent of cross-breed cows, 63 per cent of local cows and buffaloes are born at home. Since government finance is available only to cross-breed cows, 39 per cent of cross-breed cows are acquired with institutional finance. 13 per cent of cross-breed cattle are purchased with self-finance mostly at the age of one year with low cost. Local cows and buffaloes acquired with self finance/leased in have no particular trend in different regions.

Region-wise analysis reveals that 47 per cent of cross-breed cows in central region are born at home and 37 per cent are purchased with institutional finance and the remaining are acquired through self-finance and for lease.But in eastern and western regions most of the cross-breed cows are purchased with institutional finance (75 per cent and 63 per cent respectively) and cows born at home are very few.

5.15 Animals in Milk and Their Average Milk Yield

Lion share of the dairy income comes from milk production which depends on the proportion of animals in milk and their milk yield. High proportion of animals in milk with higher

Table 5.14
Mode of Acquisition of Milch animals by the Member Households

Category	Central region				Eastern region				Western region				All regions			
	Home breed	Purchased with self finance	Purchase with Govt. Asst.	Leased	Home breed	Purchased with self finance	Purchase with Govt. Asst.	Leased	Home breed	Purchased with self finance	Purchase with Govt. Asst.	Leased	Home breed	Purchased with self finance	Purchase with Govt. Asst.	Leased
Local cows	14	6	-	6	3	1	-	1	5	2	-	2	22	9	-	9
Crossbreed cows	28	10	22	8	1	-	3	-	2	-	5	1	31	10	30	9
Buffaloes	8	4	-	2	16	2	-	2	4	1	-	-	28	7	-	4
Total	50	20	22	16	20	3	3	3	11	3	5	3	81	26	30	22

milk potentiality is a pre-requisite to secure more income from dairying. The Table 5.15 provides details about animals in milk and their average milk yield.

Out of 159 total milch animals of the member households 35 animals are dry and remaining 124 are in milk,yielding 800.5 litres per year on an average. The table further shows that the proportion of animals in milk and their average milk yield among local cows, buffaloes and cross-breed cows vary widely. The proportion of animals in milk and the average milk yield of local cows and buffaloes is very much lower than cross breed cows of the member households. Of the total 80 cross-breed cows 92.5 per cent are in milk, with an average milk yield of 1042.7 litres per year.

The variation in milk yield of cross-breed cows is not an exception from regional variations since milk yield depends on climate, quality of cows, feeding practices etc.Of the three regions of the district average milk production is slightly higher in western region (1078.6 litres per annum) with good climate followed by central (1042 litres)and eastern regions (1006.5 litres).

The table further reveals that high proportion of cross-breed cows to total milch animals in a region influences the average milk yield of the region positively.Accordingly average milk yield is higher in central region(878 litres per annum) with high proportion of cross-breed cows followed by western (666 litres) and eastern region (532 litres).

5.16 Breeding Practices

There are two alternative breeding practices that are followed to breed the milch animals namely Natural Service (NS) and Artificial Insemination (AI) facility.Breeding practices followed by cattle keeping households depend on the extent and availability of infrastructure and supply of input for artificial insemination and the degree of utilisation of artificial insemination facility by cattle keeping households. Table 5.16 presents breeding practices followed by member households.

Table 5.15
Animals in Milk and Dry and their Average Milk Yield*

(Milk yield in litres)

Category	Central			Eastern			Western			All regions		
	Dry animals	*Animals in milk*	*Average milk yield*	*Dry animals*	*Animals in milk*	*Average milk yield*	*Dry animals*	*Animals in milk*	*Average milk yield*	*Dry animals*	*Animals in milk*	*Average milk yield*
Local cows	8	18	514.00	2	3	430.00	4	5	408.00	14	26	484.90
Cross breed cows	4	64	1041.60	-	4	1006.50	2	6	1078.50	6	74	1042.70
Buffaloes	5	9	437.33	8	12	399.00	2	3	270.00	15	24	397.30
Total	**17**	**91**	**877.50**	**10**	**19**	**531.80**	**8**	**14**	**665.78**	**35**	**124**	**800.50**

* Average milk yield of animals in milk.

Table 5.16
Breeding Practices followed by the Member Households

	Central region		*Eastern region*		*Western region*		*All regions*	
	AI	*NS*	*AI*	*NS*	*AI*	*NS*	*AI*	*NS*
Local cows	22	4	3	2	5	3	30	9
Cross-breed cows	66	2	4	-	8	-	78	2
Buffaloes	-	14	-	20	-	5	-	39
Total	**88**	**20**	**7**	**22**	**13**	**8**	**108**	**50**

Table shows that cattle keeping households have followed both natural service and artificial insemination practices to breed their cows. For 98 per cent of cross-breed cows and 77 per cent of local cows artificial in semination is practiced. When cross-breed cows are not conceived through AI, in few attempts, then, Natural Services is practised. For 23 per cent of local cows NS is practiced to obtain good quality of bullocks. Only NS is practiced for buffaloes with the hope that conceiving rate of AI is almost zero for local buffaloes. The breeding practices are almost similar in all the three regions of the district since AI facility is provided at milk cooperatives under operation flood programme where veterinary hospitals are not with in the reach of the member households.

5.17 Average Annual Household Expenditure on Milch Animals

Maximization of dairy income largely depends on direct input cost minimization. Since dairy farming is labour intensive it helps the poor who have extra manpower to convert their excess labour to generate additional income. Feeding of live stock amounts to over 75 per cent of total cost. Proper feeding of dairy cattle involves feeding of green grass and fodder. This is most economical and cost effective. Green grass and fodder could be collected from common lands like tank beds, canal sides, forests and from the farm of the landlords on whose farm landless labourers work. At the time of sugarcane harvest sugar cane tops are collected by the agricultural labourers at free of cost to feed their animals especially in summer. In addition to feeding the milch animals with collected green gross,fodder,they are also grazed in the fields. Feeding the milch animals with all these means involves no direct cost to the beneficiaries except labour services. The question of hired labour in dairying does not arise for agricultural labour households in the district.

Next to green fodder, dry fodders such as paddy straw groundnut halves are commonly fed to the dairy animals. Dry fodder was partly collected by the beneficiaries during the harvest time and partly used for their own crop residuals. Concentrate feeds like feed, groundnut cake,mineral mixture etc. are used at low level, to minimise direct costs by the labour households. Besides feed, the other items that accounted for cost of milk production are annual intrest, on loan,cost of animal, insurance charges if any, and depreciation on cows value.

Thus agricultural labour household expenditure on milch animals can be divided, broadly, into two categories:(1) Labour cost (imputed cost of family labour used for grazing, collection of green grass,sugarcane tops, dry fodder, bathing and shed cleaning, feeding , milking and marketing) and (2) Other than labour cost, which includes cost of concentrate feed like groundnut cake, feed, imputed cost of farm by-products, interest on investment on dairy and depreciation on cows value.

Table 5.17 presents the annual average household expenditure on milch animals of the member households.

Table 5.17
Annual Average Household Expenditure on Milch Animals of the Member Households**

Region	*Labour cost*	*Other than labour cost*	*Over all expenditure*
Central	2675.89	1142.00	3817.89
Eastern	2801.67	188.16	3989.8

(Table Contd...)

Table 5.17 (Contd...)

Western	2436.70	1005.90	3442.60
All regions	2666.88	1133.76	3800.66

** Includes cost of follower cattle.

* Family labour cost is computed based on the existing annual wages in the respective villages.

It is observed from the table that average household overall expenditure of the total member household on dairy is Rs.3801. It is highest in eastern region(Rs.3990) followed by central (Rs.3818) and western(Rs.3443) regions. It is noted from the table that labour cost accounted for 70 per cent of over all cost in all regions irrespective of variations in animal composition and average size of animal holdings. For example, in central region cross-breed cows accounted 63 per cent to total milch animals and the average size of milch animal holdings is only 1.4. Whereas in eastern region cross-breed cows accounted only 14 per cent to total and the average size of animal holding is 2.4.

It is further noted from the table that in absolute terms labour cost is more in eastern region(Rs.2802) due to existing high wages in the region followed by central region (Rs.2676) and western region (Rs.2437).

In brief household expenditure on dairy animals is highest in eastern region and lowest in western region and moderate in central region.

5.18 Gross Average Household Annual Income

Income in dairy is generated from total annual milk production, sale of the young follower or assessed value when the follower was still in possession and sale of manure.

Table reveals that average milk production per household is 987 litres per annum. Milk production per household is highest in central region (1051 litres) with highest composition of crossbreed cows followed by western(932 litres) and eastern (677 litres) regions. The average value of milk produced is

Rs.4758 for all the households and the value of milk is highest in central (Rs.4838) followed by eastern region (Rs-4490) and western region (Ra.4473). In eastern region milk value is relatively higher because of large quantity of buffalo milk production and its high price.

Table 5.18
Annual Gross Average Income per Member Household

(in rupees)

Region	*Average production per house-hold (Lts.)*	*Average value of the milk produced*	*Average value of the follower*	*Average value of the dung*	*Average gross income*
Central	1050.60	4837.79	644.74	260.00	5742.53
Eastern	877.80	4490.33	433.00	439.50	5446.50
Western	932.10	4472.70	640.00	237.50	5350.20
All regions	987.14	4757.99	618.33	279.68	5666.25

Note: In 1992 year prices.

5.19 Net Annual Income from Dairy

The net annual dairy income of the member households is computed on the basis of total value of milk produced. The valuation for milk is made on the basis of sale price received by the milk producers from dairy cooperatives. The sale price for all cooperative members is same in all regions with slight variation depending on the quality of milk supplied. But sale price of buffalo milk is higher than cow milk. The net income is arrived at after deducting the value of milk consumed at home and expenditure on the dairy animals. Table 5.19 presents the net annual dairy income of the sample households.

From the table it is observed that the value of milk consumption at home per total households is only Rs.538. To say, milk consumption of the member households is nominal since they keep milk at home mainly to feed infants and to prepare butter milk for rare consumption. Consumption of tea,coffee,milk, is occasional practices in all the regions. When milk consumption is nominal, net dairy income depends on gross income and over all expenditure on dairy.The table shows that average net dairy income per household is Rs.1328 and it varies from region to region. Net dairy income is highest in western region (Rs.1443) followed by central region (Rs.1367) and eastern region (Rs.985).

Table 5.19
Net Annual Dairy Income of the Member Households (in Rs)

Region	*Gross income*	*Value of milk consumed at home*	*Overall expenditure*	*Net income*
Central	5742.53	557.63	3817.90	1367.00
Eastern	5446.50	471.17	3989.80	985.53
Western	5350.20	464.70	3442.60	1442.90
All regions	5666.25	537.56	3800.65	1328.04

5.20 Actual Dairy Income

Labour households employed family labour, mostly their leisure hours, in dairy and earned additional income to promote their living standards. For family labour no price is charged directly. In view of this actual dairy income is computed to analyse the impact of dairy on member households in another direction. In other words, actual dairy income is the sum of net dairy income plus imputed family labour cost in dairy.

Table 5.20 indicates that average annual actuval income from dairy of the households is Rs.3991 which is three times higher than net dairy income (see table 5.19). Since other than labour costs accounted only 30 percent of total cost for all regions and value of milk consumed is also minimum naturally, actual dairy income from dairy is much higher than net dairy income. It is observed from the table that actual dairy income is highest in central region (Rs.4043) followed by western (Rs.3880)and eastern regions (Ra.3787).

Table 5.20
Annual Income of the Member Households

(in Rs.)

Region	*Gross income*	*Value of milk consumed at home*	*Annual expenditure other than labour*	*Annual average actual dairy income*
Central	5742.53	557.63	1142.00	4042.90
Eastern	5446.50	571.17	1188.16	3787.17
Western	5350.20	464.70	1005.90	3879.60
All regions	5666.25	537.56	1137.60	3991.10

5.21 Employment Generation in Dairy

Dairying is a labour intensive enterprise. Rich farmers employed mostly hired labour but in the case of agricultural labour households only family labour utilised in dairy activities. The quantum of additional employment generation in dairy depends upon various factors like number and type of animals possessed, size of land holdings,irrigation facilities, cropping pattern, economic status of the households and feeding practices.

For example, a household with more number of milchanimals should work more hours than a household with less number of animals. Similarly, a household with cross breed animals required more labour for feeding, and to clean them. A household with irrigated land required few labour hours to feed animals with farm grown fodder and crop residuals whereas land less labour should spend more hours to collect green grass and fodder from tank beds, common lands or from others land and for grazing the animals.

Further dairying is a collective activity of the entire family. No single member is exclusively engaged in dairy cattle activity. In this activity entire family members contribute their labour for collection of feed and fodder and marketing of milk. The Table 5.21 presents employment generation in dairy for men, women and children of the households.

Table 5.21
Employment Generation in Dairy for the Sample Households Per Annum

(in days)

Region	*Men*	*Women*	*Children*	*Total*	*Average*	*Mandays hours per day*
Central	73.6	140.5	50.8	264.9	5.8	204.4
Eastern	46.7	131.7	75.8	254.2	5.6	183.3
Western	59.5	140.2	71.0	270.7	5.7	200.2
All regions	68.9	139.4	55.9	264.2	5.8	201.4

As shown in the table on an average men are working 69 days, women 140 days and children 56 days in dairy activities by the member households. The table further reveals that women participation in dairy activities is much higher (52.8 per cent) than men (26 per cent) and children(21.2 per cent).

Region wise analysis shows that collective working days of men, women and children are more in western region(271 days) followed by central region (265 days) and eastern region (254 days). Next to women, children are working more days in eastern and western regions where as in central region men are working more days than children. The table further shows that, on an average a household spent 5.8 hours collectively for different dairy activities and the regional variations are negligible.

In the study area since the wages of woman and children wages are nearly three-fourths and one-half of wage of man, the working days of woman and children working days are converted into mandays in the same proportion. This analysis shows that the dairy generated an additional employment of 201 mandays per household and it varies from region to region. In central region additional employment generation in dairy is 204 man days followed by western region (200 mandays) and eastern region (183 mandays).

To sum up in terms of mandays, additional employment generation in dairy is highest in cross-breed cows dominated central region and lowest in eastern region where the proportion of local cows and buffaloes are high. Western region stands in between these two regions.

5.22 Break-up of Employment

In dairying labour is required mainly to graze animals, collection of gross, fodder and for cleaning of animals, shed cleaning, feeding, milking and milk marketing operations. These operations are collectively done by the entire family members. Duration of these operations vary in relation to type of animals possessed, animals in milk or dry, availability of grass,fodder and climate. For example, local animals are grazed more hours than cross-breed cows. Cross-breed animals especially cows in milk are grazed minimum hours and fed with collected grass and fodder and crop residual. Similarly in summer green grass is not available in common lands so that animals are fed with crop residuals and feed. The table 5.22 provides the particulars about the average time spent for different dairy activities per day.

Table 5.22
Break-up of Employment in Dairy of the Member Household

(hours per day)

Sl. No.	*Operation*	*Central region*	*Eastern region*	*Western region*	*All regions*
1.	Grazing	2.5	4.1	2.9	2.7
2.	Collection of grass sugarcane tops	2.1	0.5	2.2	1.9
3.	Bathing and shed cleaning	0.6	0.4	0.4	0.6
4.	Feeding, milking & milk marketing	0.6	0.6	0.4	0.6
	Total	**5.8**	**5.6**	**5.9**	**5.8**

As shown in Table 5.22, on an average, a household spent 5.8 hours for different dairy activities. Activity wise, the major work is grazing the animals (2.7 hours)followed by green grass, sugarcane tops collection(1.9 hours). For the remaining two categories of activitie's only 0.6 hours each are spent by a household.

The time spent for grazing the animals and for grass collection vary from region to region. The average time spent per day for grazing is more in eastern region(4.1 hours) where local cows and buffaloes are more followed by western region (2.9 hours) and central region (2.5 hours)The average time spent for collection of grass and sugarcane tops is 2.2 hours in western region, 2.1 hours in central region and only 0.5 hours in eastern region. The time spent for other activities are almost same in all regions.

In brief, though total time spent for dairy activity is almost same in all the regions, the time spent for grazing and gross collection varies from region to region mainly in proportion with the composition of cross-breed and local animals.

Section-III : Poverty Dimensions of Sample Households

The section deals with income composition, income distribution and poverty dimensions of the sample member and non-member households.

5.23 Income Composition of Sample Households

Rural households earned income from various sources viz., farming, livestock like sheep,goat and bullocks, dairying, poultry, agricultural wage employment,non-agricultural wage employment, business etc. Table 5.23 presents the income composition of sample households.

Table 5.23
Income Composition of the Sample Households

(in Rs.)

Sl. No.	*Source of income*	*Central region*	*Eastern region*	*Western region*	*All regions*
1.	Agricultural wage	6593.33	8491.45	6161.17	6999.32
2.	Dairy	998.96	190.74	240.48	575.86

(Table Contd...)

Table 5.23 (Contd...)

3.	Farm	1198.12	760.48	1001.08	1025.75
4.	Livestock*	314.42	378.31	700.08	434.34
5.	Others	563.44	346.77	832.92	565.55
	Total	**9668.27**	**10167.75**	**8935.73**	**9610.82**

* Sheep,goat and bullocks.

Table 5.23 reveals that average income of the total sample households is Rs.9611 per annum. Average income in eastern region is highest with Rs.10168 followed by central region (Rs.9668) and western region (Rs.8936). The share of agricultural wage to total income is 73 per cent for total sample households and it varies from 83.5 per cent in eastern region to 68 per cent in central region depending on wage rate, work participation and nature of employment.Dairy contribution is 6 per cent of total households income and it varies from 10 per cent in central region to 2 percent in eastern region. Farm income accounts 11 per cent of total household income and it varies from 12.4 per cent in central region to 7.4 per cent in eastern region. Livestock(sheep,goat and bullocks) contribution is 4.5 per cent of total income and it ranges from 7.8 per cent in western region to 3.3 per cent in central region. And other sources like petty business, non-farm employment etc., added 6 percent to the total households income and it varies from 9.3 per cent in western region to 3.4 per cent in eastern region. In brief, the table shows that major share of income of the sample households come from agricultural wage employment followed by farming, dairying, non farm employment and live stock. Though agricultural wage employment is the main sources of income in all regions, the proportion of other incomes to their respective total incomes vary from region to region and even within the region between members and non-members.

5.24 Income Composition of Member and Non-member Households

Table 5.24 presents the income composition of member and non-member households. Average income of the member household is Rs.9756 and non-member household is Rs.9500. Income composition of member and non-member varies significantly. Agricultural wage accounted for 67 per cent for members and 78 per cent for non-members. Dairy income accounted 14 per cent for members. Since non-members have no dairy cattle they won't have dairy income. Farm income accounted for 11 and 10 per cent for members and non-members income respectively. The composition of livestock income is more to the non-members and less to the members i-e.,6 percent and 2.6 per cent respectively. And non-farm income accounted 5.6 per cent for members and 6.3 per cent for non-members. In brief, in absence of dairy the share of wage and livestock income to total income of the non-member house-holds is higher than member households in all regions.

5.25 Income Distribution

Table 5.25 presents the per capita monthly income particulars of the sample households. It reveals that of the 226 sample households, 66 households (29.2 per cent) per capita income is Rs.150 and below, 89 households (39.4 per cent) percapita is in between Rs.150 and 200 and remaining 71 households (31.4 per cent) per capita is above 200. The proportion of households among different per capita in come groups varies in between members and non-member households and among different regions. Of the total (98 member and 126 non-member households), 61 per cent of member and 74 percent of non-member households per capita income is Rs.200 and below and remaining households monthly per capita income is above Rs.200. The table further reveals that the proportion of households with monthly per capita Rs.200 and below are more in non-member households than member households in all regions.

5.26 Poverty Dimensions Among Sample Households

To estimate absolute poverty, income approach as well as expenditure approach is followed. In this study income approach is followed by taking Planning Commissions poverty

Table 5.24
Income Composition of the Sample Households
(Members and Non-members)

(Average annual income in Rs.)

Source	Central Region		Eastern Region		Western Region		All Regions	
	Members	*Non-Members*	*Members*	*Non-Members*	*Members*	*Non-Members*	*Members*	*Non-Members*
Agricultural wage	6388.37	7149.64	7800.00	8657.40	6132.00	6167.00	6535.06	7354.77
Dairy	1367.00	-	985.50	-	1442.90	-	1328.03	-
Farm	1220.84	1136.43	670.83	782.00	669.00	1067.00	1097.18	971.05
Livestock*	215.79	582.14	425.00	367.10	330.50	774.00	253.11	573.08
Others	563.16	564.29	333.33	350.00	635.00	872.50	542.35	600.98
Total	**9755.16**	**9432.50**	**10214.63**	**10156.50**	**9209.40**	**8881.00**	**9755.73**	**9499.88**

* Sheep,goat and bullocks.

Note: Income refers net income from each source.

Table 5.25

Distraction of Monthly per Capita Income of Member and Non-members Sample Households

Income group Central region Eastern region Western region All regions

Members Non-members Members Non-members Members N o n - members Members Non-members

Income group	Central Region		Eastern Region		Western Region		All region	
	Members	*Non-Members*	*Members*	*Non-Members*	*Members*	*Non-Members*	*Members*	*Non-Members*
0-100	-	2	-	-	-	5	-	7
100-150	16	10	2	7	3	21	21	38
150-200	34	12	3	22	2	16	39	50
200-250	18	4	5	18	4	8	27	30
250 & Above	8	-	2	3	1	-	11	3
Total	**76**	**28**	**12**	**50**	**10**	**50**	**98**	**128**

$$\text{Percapita household income} = \frac{\text{Average net family income per month}}{\text{No.of persons in respective households}}.$$

Note: $$\text{Percapita household income} = \frac{\text{household income including imputed family labour costs}}{\text{family size}}.$$

line definition. The poverty line so defined was Rs.49.10 for rural areas in the base year 1973-74. The same poverty line is updated for the year 1992-93 by using agricultural labour price index. On this basis monthly per capita income of Rs.168.84 is derived as poverty line for the study. The table 5.26 depicts the poverty dimensions of the sample households.

Table 5.26
Poverty Among Sample Households

	Member households		*Non-Member households*		*Total households*	
Region	*House-holds in poverty*	*Persons in poverty*	*House-holds in poverty*	*Persons in poverty*	*House-holds in poverty*	*Persons in poverty*
Central	24	108	16	80	4	188
Eastern	2	10	10	45	12	55
Western	5	26	30	170	35	196
All regions	31	144	56	295	87	439

Table shows that out of 226 sample households 87 households i.e., 38 per cent, are in poverty and the percentage of households in poverty are more in western region (58 per cent) followed by central region (38 per cent) and eastern region (19 per cent). Similarly out of 1034 sample population 42.5 per cent i.e., 439 persons are in poverty and the percentage of population below poverty line is highest in western region (68 per cent) followed by central region (38 per cent) and eastern region (24 percent). The proportion of poor households and poor population not only differ from region to region but also from member households to non-member households. The table further shows that percentages of poor households as well as poor persons below poverty line are more among non-member households than member households in all the regions.

The table shows that, 31.5 per cent of member and 57 per cent of non-member households in central region, 17 per cent of member and 20 per cent of non-member households in eastern region and 50 per cent of member and 60 per cent of non-member households in western region are in poverty.In terms of population 31 per cent and 58 per cent in central region, 20 and 22 per cent in eastern region and 59 and 69 per cent in western region are poor among member and non-member households respectively. In total 32 per cent of persons among member and 50 per cent among non-member households are in poverty.

In terms of percentages poor among non-member households is 18 per cent higher than member households and it varies from region to region. The poor among non-member households are 27 per cent higher than member households in central region followed by western region (10 per cent)and eastern region (2 per cent).

5.27 Sen 'P' Measure as the Basis of Monthly Per Capita Income Distribution

Head count ratio method is the common procedure adopted to count the number of the poor and check the percentage of the total population belonging to this category. All the households below the poverty line are not equally poor. The head count ratio method does not take into consideration about the short fall in income by which the households fall below the poverty line. This is taken into account in the poverty measure 'P'[97] suggested by Sen. According to Sen `P' measure is not concerned merely with the number of people below the poverty line but also with the amounts by which the incomes of the poor fall short of the specified poverty line. The greater the short fall from the poverty level, the greater is the weight per unit of that short fall in poverty measure.

Table 5.27 presents sen 'P' mesure as the basis of monthly per capita income distribution of the sample households. It reveals that of the total sample population 42.5 per cent are poor and their average monthly per capita income is Rs. 131.54. The poverty measure 'P' which refers short fall of income below poverty line is 0.188. The table further shows that the percentage of people below poverty line are greater (50 per cent) in non-

Table 5.27
Sen 'P' Measure as the Basis of Per Capita Distribution of Income

Sl. No	Income group	Central region			Eastern region			Western region			All regions		
		Member house holds	Non-member house holds	Total house holds	Member hhouse holds olds	Non-member house holds	Total house holds	Member house holds olds	Non-member house holds	Total house holds	Member house holds olds	Non-member house holds	Total house holds olds
1.	Proportion of persons below poverty line	30.7	58.00	38.36	20.00	22.00	21.60	59.00	69.40	67.80	32.30	50.20	42.50
2.	Average per capita income of persons below poverty line	136.55	130.17	133.60	140.20	138.10	138.48	135.20	126.44	127.60	136.25	129.23	131.54
3.	Poverty measure 'P'	0.119	0.266	0.158	0.068	0.080	0.078	0.236	0.349	0.331	0.125	0.235	0.1876

member households than member households (32.3 per cent) and the 'P' value is also higher for non-member households (0.235) than member households (0.125) in the study area.

The table further states that the percentage of people below poverty line as well as the value of 'P' is lower (0.078) in eastern region followed by central region (0.158). In western region the percentage of poor as well as the 'P' value is higher (0.331). Again within the regions the value of 'P' is lower for member households and higher for non-member households.

Thus the proportion of poor and poverty measure 'P' is higher in western region followed by central and eastern regions. Similarly the proportion of poor and poverty measure 'P' value is greater among non-member households than member households.

In brief, though operation flood programme does not solve the problem of poverty totally among member households it succeeded in reduction of intensity of poverty considerably especially in central region and western regions where more poor are sheltered. Thus the study supports the hypothesis that dairy development in Chittoor district has helped agricultural labour households to mitigate poverty.

5.28 Poverty Dimensions : Actual Dairy Income Criteria

The table presents the extent of poverty among sample households based on actual dairy income criteria.

The table shows that of the total member households 10.2 households and 12.3 per cent of their population are in poverty. It is noteworthy that based on actual dairy income criteria the incidence of poverty has come down to the minimum because actual dairy income is three times higher than net dairy income (refer Table 5.20).

The table further reveals that poverty is absent in eastern region and in central and western regions the incidence of poverty has come down to 12.5 per cent and 25 per cent respectively. As shown in the table poverty measure 'P' is only

0.0138 for total member households. Further the poverty measure 'P' is quite low in central region (0.0125) than western region (0.0425). The study reveals that when family labour income from dairy is added to the total household income many agricultural labour households, who are members of the milk cooperatives, incidence of poverty is considerably reduced.

Thus it can be inferred that the dairy development through operation Flood programme has significant impact on agricultural labourer's poverty in general, and in central and western regions in particular.

Table 5.28
Poverty Among Member Households
Based on Actual Dairy Income Criteria

Region	*Total house-holds*	*House holds below poverty*	*Total No.of persons*	*Persons below poverty line*	*Average per capita monthly income of persons below poverty line (Rs)*	*Poverty measure "P"*
Central	76	8	352	44	160.4	0.0125
Eastern	12	0	50	0	-	-
Western	10	2	44	11	155.2	0.0425
All regions	98	10	446	55	159.36	0.01380

5.29 Summary

The primary data is collected from 128 non-member and 98 member sample households of the three regions. The data reveals that socio-economic conditions, agricultural wage rates, working conditions vary from region to region. Livestock - goat/sheep and bullocks are owned by sample households in the three regions but at different proportions. All milch animal owned households in the study area are enrolled as members of the milk cooperatives.

The sample households possess 159 dairy animals of which 50 per cent are cross - breed cows followed by local cows and buffaloes (25 per cent each). Since institutional finance is provided only for cross-breed cows, 39 per cent of cross breed cows are purchased with it and remaining animals are acquired through various means. Dairy income depends mostly on quantity of milk produced and on the expenditure made in dairy, which are subject to changes from region to region. Income composition of households differ not only from region to region but also between members and non-members. The poverty analysis reveals that operation Flood programme has an impact on the poverty of member households at varying degrees in different regions.

6

SUMMARY AND CONCLUSIONS

The test of our progress is not whether we add more to the abundance of those who have much; it is whether we provide enough for those who have too little.

— *F.D. Roosevelt*

Poverty is as old as society but systematic writing and research about poverty is largely a post war phenomenon. It is after Keynesian revolution poverty is viewed in terms of social origin and causation rather than individual inhibitions and inadequacies; and the national and international efforts are directed to increase the productivity of poor by knowing the fact that poverty any where is a danger to prosperity every where.

Today poverty is viewed in absolute terms rather than relative terms. The bulk of poor, about 85 per cent, are in rural areas. The rural poor includes large number of the landless as well as tenants, agricultural producers with small holdings and the people who depend on rural non-farm activities. Agricultural workers and landless whose employment is seasonal are among the poorest members of the country.

The poverty in India is no new discovery. This becomes clear even to a casual observer who roams over any part of the vast country. Inspite of the rich natural resource endowment and herculean resource mobilisation effort to reduce poverty under five year plans, India today classified as one of the worst poverty stricken nations of the world with one third of the world poor. Since 80 per cent of poor are in rural areas there is need to understand the nature and dimensions of rural poverty in India. In this book an attempt is made towards this goal.

In India there are a number of poverty estimates by the individuals, research institutions, government and international organisations. There is no dearth in this regard. But the main limitation of individual and institutional research studies are of using independent poverty parameters, as a result comparisons are not feasible.

The planning Commission has been preparing poverty estimates from time to time basing on the concept of poverty line recommended by 'Task Force' on projection of Minimum needs and effective Consumption Demand and data on household expenditure obtained through National Sample Survey Rounds. Similarly Expert Group appointed by the Planning Commission estimated poverty by making use of the same procedure but with state specific price indices. Expert Group poverty estimates show a higher incidence of poverty in India than Planning Commission estimates. But both Planning Commission and Expert Group confirmed a steady decline in the incidence of poverty in India.

Dandekar and Rath (1971) and Mahendra Dev (1988) analysed the incidence of poverty among agricultural labour households for the two periods i.e. 1956-57 and 1977-78 respectively by making use of National Sample Survey data on household expenditure. For both the studies the same poverty line concept was used. These two studies revealed that incidence of poverty among agricultural labour households has decreased for a period of twenty years, but the decrease is 'only one per cent'.

The series of Rural Labour Enquiry Reports reveals that the proportion of agricultural labour households to rural households has been increasing along with the increase in total rural households. The incidence of poverty among agricultural labour households is almost constant. This tendency confirms that the percentage of agricultural labourers among rural poor has been increasing irrespective of decreasing tendency of rural poverty in India. Hence poverty elimination can not be achieved without uplifting the poor agricultural labourers.

To improve the quality of life of all the citizens especially, to protect disadvantaged group by solving their basic problem, namely, poverty, Central and State Governments have launched numerous direct antipoverty programmes. The Sixth Five Year Plan (1980-85) sets the alternative targets one refer the incidence of poverty without redistributive measure (41 per cent) and another refer to the incidence of poverty with effective implementation of redistributive measures (30 per cent) for the year 1984-85 with the hope that effective implementation of anti-poverty programmes can reduce the incidence of poverty considerability. Through effective implementation of redistributive measures inequality in consumption expenditure has come down to 0.18 from 0.38 in between 1977-78 and 1983. But the incidence of poverty has come down only to 40 per cent instead of 30 per cent as projected by the Sixth Plan.

Thus the phenomenon indicates that mere redistributive measures alone cannot solve the incidence of poverty in near future. This under scores the need for rapid growth of output and employment coupled with strengthening of special programmes of poverty alleviation and employment generation. The problem of poverty has to be dealt in the frame work of the strategy of development laying emphasis on those sectors whose growth makes a significant impact on the income levels of the under employed. One such sector is dairy industry through which poverty problem can be solved effectively. In the book this aspect is examined systematically using secondary and primary data.

Cattle and buffaloes have been an integral part of crop-live stock system in Indian farm economy for thousands of years. In the world today, India claims first position in possessing of bovines and second position in milk production.

But India ranked 57th in the world in terms of per capita milk availability due to numerous human population in India. In 1991 per capita per day, availability of milk is 174 grams as compared to the minimum nutritional requirement of 250 grams recommended by the Indian Council of Medical Research. The gap between requirement and availability of milk and milk products can be bridged by an aggressive cattle and buffalo development programme, it comprehensively organised and effectively implemented. Government of India appointed several committees to examine the potentiality for cattle development and suggest measures to promote bovine economy since beginning of the century. All these examinations indicate tremendous potentiality for cattle development in India for rapid economic growth and desirable social changes.

On the lines of Committees recommendations Government of India introduced different schemes for promotion of bovine livestock like, key village scheme, Intensive Cattle Development Programme, Promotion of Artificial Insemination Facilities.

Organised dairying commenced in India towards the end of 19th century to supply milk to the army. Since then government appointed several dairy experts to review the position of dairying in India and to give their recommendations. During the first three five year plans the dairy development programme was initiated in a relatively small way as funds were made available only out of over all savings from other sectors.

In 1962, the government of India constituted a working group to study the prospects of dairy development and animal husbandry through cooperative organisation. The group recommended that dairy development should be attempted through cooperative lines and recommended steps for implementing this policy. Government of India set up National Dairy Development Board (NDDB) in 1965 and this Board formulated and implemented the Operation Flood (OF) Programmes in 1970 with the financial assistance of EEC and world food programme.

The OF programme has implemented in three phases. In the first phase the emphasis is to promote on the economic basis of small and marginal farmers and agricultural labourers. The second phase aimed at bringing much wider areas under this programme and envisaged a fundamental transformation of the livestock and dairy sector in India. Third phase, which is implemented upto 1994 launched to achieve a strong and self sustainable cooperative dairy sector in India.

Thus in response to Government efforts the dairy sector of the country has witnessed a change especially in the last two decades. The per capita milk availability has gone up from 110 grams in 1973 to 174 grams in 1990. All these achievements could be well attributed largely to the operation Flood programme.

In India dairying is a small man's enterprise. Small man maintains one or two milch animals on crop residues and by-products with under employed family labour, mostly female work force. Rainfed lands face great instability in crop production but these lands sustain livestock better than crop production. Hence livestock production has been found to provide economic stability to the farmers residing in rainfed areas.

In any assessment of dairy development has to be taken not only of its impact in promotion of milk production in the country but also of social impact particularly on the rural poor who produce the milk. There are several studies giving conflicting evidences on the impact of Operation Flood programme. But majority of the studies reveal that Operation Flood is sound in uplifting rural masses above the poverty by generating additional employment and income.

Chittoor district has a pride of place in dairying in Andhra Pradesh. Operation Flood is a grand success in Chittoor district. As per National Dairy Development Board appraisal report 1990, Chittoor milk union procured about one-fourth of milk procurement of Andhra Pradesh. For these reasons Chittoor district is selected for the study.

Since the district is subject to wide regional variations with regard to climate, rainfall, irrigation, soil, livestock possession, an attempt is made to analyse the impact of dairy development through Operation Flood programme in promotion of milk procurement in three regions of the district.

The district is part of drought-prone-Rayalaseema region. It covers an extent of 15152 sq.km. and has 32.5 lakh population of which 80 per cent are rural. In the district agricultural labour accounts for 35 per cent of total work force (1990-91). NSS estimates (1977-78) reveal that 53 per cent of rural people are living below poverty line and the incidence of poverty of agricultural labour is 72 per cent.

The district has the benefit of receiving rainfall during the south-west and north-east monsoons. In the district 32 per cent of geographical area is left for cultivation and this comparatively small cultivated area is unequally distributed. In absence of any major river, tanks and wells constitute the chief source of irrigation. Food crops account for 44 per cent of total cropped area and the rest is under commercial crops.

The district has comparatively large number of cattle but accounts less buffaloes. In this district cattle development was taken up as early as 1958 through key village schemes. In 1975-76 Intensive Cattle Development Programme was initiated under Drought Prone Area Programme (DPAP) to intensify cross-breed programme. The district obtained the credit as the best district in the state for implementing cross-breed work. As a result Government selected this district to implement Pregnancy Testing programme. Further to provide animal health cover and breeding facility to interior rural areas, Animal Husbandry Mobile Inputs and Ambulatory Scheme was introduced under DPAP. In addition to this under OF-II and OF-III technical inputs programme was implemented for selected Dairy Cooperatives to protect animal health, provide artificial insemination facility etc. Central Government sponsored Special Livestock Breeding Programme to assist agricultural laburers, small,marginal farmers in livestock production and to generate additional employment and income and to bring them above poverty line. Secondary data analysis shows that Chittoor dairy has made rapid development. Milk procurement has maintained a positive increasing trend which is statistically significant. Marketing of milk has also registered statistically significant increasing trend.

The provision of good institutional and infrastructural facilities in addition to peoples attitude in promotion of improved livestock have led to increase the size of cross breed cattle surprisingly. The density of cross-breed cow population in 1987 was 10 per sq.km. in the district comparatively much higher than Rayalaseema (3) and Andhra Pradesh (1). But cross-breed programme through artificial insemination facility for buffaloes is a failure in the district.

Since the district is not an exception for regional variations, the general features of the district need not necessarily resemble in all the regions. The district has been divided into three natural divisions, namely Central, Eastern and Western regions. The central region with moderate climate consists of 12 mandals or 16 per cent of district's geographical area. The eastern region comprising 23 mandals of plains in the east accounted for 30 per cent of geographical area. The western region with 31 mandals of uplands,hillocks accounted for 54 per cent of geographical area. Hence stratified multistage sampling design is used to select sample households.

Various socio-economic dimensions of rural poverty are examined with the help of primary data.

In western region density of population is much less than the other two regions; it accounts by only half of the eastern region. Central region stands in-between eastern and western regions. Though the proportion of agricultural labourers to main workers is almost same in all regions the proportion of female labour to male labour varies from region to region. The proportion of female labour per thousand male labour is highest in western region (994) followed by eastern region (870) and central region (766).

In the district regional variations are more visible with regard to cropping pattern. In eastern region due to north east monsoon 59 per cent of crops are grown under rabi season. In contrast, in western region 92 per cent of crops are grown in Kharif, because of south-west monsoon. In central region 86 per cent of crops are grown in Kharif season. In eastern region paddy is the principle crop (41 per cent) followed by groundnut (38.9 per cent). In western region groundnut as a dry crop is the principle crop (60 per cent of total cropped area) followed by paddy (14 per cent). Central region has some special features. Here 54 per cent of total cropped area is under groundnut followed by sugarcane (14 per cent) mango (10 per cent) and Paddy (10 per cent).

Like cropping pattern the extent of irrigation also varies from region to region considerably. In eastern region more than three-fourths of gross cropped area is irrigated followed by central and western regions with meager 31 and 23 per cent respectively. Thus agriculture in western and central regions mostly depends on nature unlike eastern region.

On an average every 100 acres of cropped area in the district sustained with 98 bovine - comprising 80 cattle and 18 buffaloes. But significant disparities are observed in the stocking rates. The central region has the highest bovine density (137) followed by eastern region (131) and western region (73). But cross-breed cattle are mostly concentrated in central region (41) followed by eastern region (7) and western region (6). It is note worthy here that 58 per cent of total cross breed cattle are in central region. Further, the composition of buffaloes and cattle presents another dimension. In eastern region buffaloes account more than half of the bovine population and accounts 57 per cent of total buffaloes in the district. In other regions buffaloes accounted only 10 to 14 per cent of their respective cattle population.

In 1969 Chittoor dairy unit was started at Chittoor under Intensive Milk Supply Scheme and in 1975 it was undertaken by Dairy Development Corporation. Further in 1981 dairy unit was included as part of OF-II. Under OF-II Rs. 486.05 lakhs and under OF-III Rs. 859 lakhs was sanctioned under different heads. To popularize dairying in the entire district 5 milk chilling centres were started since 1977. In central region milk products factory is situated. Two milk chilling centres are in eastern region and remaining three are in western region. The handling capacity of milk products factory and milk chilling centres of western region are enhanced many times. But milk chilling centres handling capacity in eastern region has not been enhanced, because the milk procurement is lower than initial installed handling capacity.

In 1970-71 Chittoor dairy procured only 9 lakhs litres of milk and by 1980-81 it reached to 173 lakh litres. After inclusion of milk shed under OF-II, dairy activities are intensified as a result 727 lakh litres are procured during 1989-90.

Anand pattern milk cooperative frame work is the vital instrument in Operation Flood programme. In the district there are 889 milk cooperatives covered 12 per cent of rural households as members. It is to note that 64 per cent of total milk cooperatives are in central region, where 58 per cent of cross breed population of the district is concerntrated and covered 39 per cent of total rural households followed by western region and eastern regions.

In view of the grand success of Operation Flood programme an attempt is made to study the impact of dairy development through Operation Flood Programme in agricultural labour households in three regions of the district. For the study 20 milk cooperatives are chosen randomly in proportion to the total cooperatives of the respective regions. From each one of the selected milk cooperatives 10 per cent of member households and non-member households are selected randomly which forms the sample of our investigation.

The analysis of socio-economic conditions of the sample households reveals that in all regions around 90 per cent of agricultural labour households belong to socially backward classes but literacy rate varies from region to region. Literacy rate is lower in economically backward wester region (34 per cent) followed by central region (37 per cent) and some what higher in eastern region (53.5 per cent). The main workers are more in eastern delta region (50.5 per cent) with fair employment opportunities and lower in western region (42.6 per cent) due to lack of employment opportunities. In western region marginal workers accounted 23 per cent which is much higher than other two regions. Similarly average size of household is bigger (4.8) in this backward region and smaller in other two regions. The size of operational holdings are larger in western rainfed region (152 cents) where the density of population and irrigation facilities are lower followed by central region (66 cents) and eastern region (64 cents) respectively.

Agricultural labour households earn some additional income through sheep/goat rearing and by maintaining bullocks for ploughing. In the drought-prone western region 25 per cent of households possess sheep/goat followed by central region (20 per cent) and eastern region (8 per cent). In eastern region where regular employment is available for bullocks 44 per cent of households own bullocks followed by western region (37 per cent) and central region (12 per cent). In central region maintaining milch animals is profitable than bullocks thus very less number of households owned bullocks.

Wage constitutes the major source of income to the agricultural households, and it depends on number of working days and the existing wage rates in the villages or region. The average working days for male is highest in sugarcane growing central region (161 days) followed by eastern region (158 days) and low in western region (142 days). In contrast, female working days are slightly higher in western region than other two regions. The agricultural wages for male and female are much higher in irrigated eastern region followed by central region and wage rates are very much low in western region. For example, average wage rates for male is Rs. 21, Rs. 18 and Rs. 16 in eastern, central and western regions respectively. Naturally wage earnings per worker is more in eastern region followed by other two regions.

In contrast to agricultural wage rates, hours of work for agricultural operations is very much less in eastern region due to more demand for labour followed by central region. In western region where the demand for labour is very less, workers are forced to work more hours so as to get some what regular employment. For example the duration of sowing operation is 6.5 hours in eastern region, 8.5 hours in central region but 9.5 hours in western region. Thus, in western and central regions wage rates are comparatively low but working hours are more.

In the study area all dairy animal owned agricultural labour households enrolled as members of milk cooperatives to get attractive benefits like bonus, regular payment for milk, subsidised feed. The total sample households (98) owned 159 milch animals of which 50 per cent are cross breed cows followed by local cows and buffaloes (25 per cent each). The composition of local, cross breed cows, buffaloes vary from region to region depending upon climate, geographical conditions, degree of successful implementation of cattle development programmes accessibility of institutional finance etc. The proportion of cross breed cows is more (63 per cent) than local cows and buffaloes in central region because of successful implementation of cattle development programmes, especially Artificial Insemination (AI) facility. The composition of buffaloes are more numerous (69 per cent) in eastern delta region which is more suitable for buffaloes. Local cows population is high (41 per cent) in mountain plateau (western region) than cross breed cows and buffaloes.

Depending on the composition of milch animals average size of cattle holdings also vary from region to region. In cross breed cows dominated central region average size of holding is (1.4) lower than eastern reagin (2.4) and western region (2.8). Since government finance is available to cross breed cows alone agricultural labour availed institutional finance to purchase cross breed cows only. Other category of milch animals are acquired with self finance or for lease or in the form of gifts etc.

Artificial insemination facility is commonly used for cross breed cows and local cows in all regions but only Natural

Service method followed for buffaloes with the hope that AI has not yielded good results.

Agricultural labour households expenditure on milch animals can be divided broadly into two categories namely labour cost (Imputed Cost of family labour) and other than labour cost. Family labour is used for grazing the animals, collection of grass,fodder, bathing and shed cleaning, feeding, milking and milk marketing purposes. No hired labour is employed.

In all the regions almost same number of hours per day are spared for dairy activities. But the time spent for grazing is more (4.1 hours) in eastern region and the time spent for collection of grass is very less (0.5 hours) because buffaloes and local cows are mostly fed by crop residuals rather than collected grass. In central region grazing hours are less (2.56) because cross breed cows are grazed less number of hours and they are fed with collected green grass,fodder. In western region milch animals are grazed for 2.9 hours and 2.2 hours time is spent for collection of grass. The time spent for other dairy activities are almost same in all the regions.

Since dairy is a collective activity of the entire family members, no single member is exclusively engaged in dairy. In all regions women participation is dominant (50 per cent) followed by children and men.

It terms of man days dairy generated 204 days employment per year in central region followed by western region (200 days) and eastern region (183 days). On an average dairy generated 201 days employment for member households in the study area.

Labour cost accounted for 70 per cent of household expenditure on milch animals in all regions irrespective of size and composition of animal holdings. But in absolute terms labour cost vary from region to region depending on the prevailing annual wage rates. Household expenditure on dairy is highest in eastern region followed by central region. In drought-prone western region dairy costs are very much less.

The main source of dairy income is quantity of milk produced. The other sources are value of the follower cattle and dung value. Though average milk produced per household is 987 litres in all regions, average milk production is highest in central region (1051 litres) followed by western (932 litres) and eastern (877) regions. Since in all regions the household consumption of milk is nominal net dairy income mostly depends on the gross income and total cost on dairy. The net dairy income per household is more in western region due to low wage rates. Central region stands second in this respect. In eastern region net income is low because of high labour costs and low milk production due to possession of more local buffaloes.

Agricultural households earn income from various sources like agricultural wage employment, dairy farming, livestock, petty business and non-farm employment. However, major source of income for member and non-member households is the agricultural wage in the study area. Agricultural wage income accounted 67 per cent for members and 78 per cent for non-members in total. Dairy income accounted 14 per cent for member households and there is no dairy income for non-members. Farm income accounted 11 and 10 per cent for member and non-member households. The share of livestock (excluding dairy) income is more (6 per cent) to the non-member households than member households (2 per cent). Non farm income account for 5.6 per cent for members and 6.3 per cent for non-members. In brief, in absence of dairy, the share of wages and livestock income to total income of the non-member households is higher than member household. The average annual income for member households in the study area is Rs. 9756 and for non-member households it is Rs. 9500. In other words dairying generated an additional income of Rs. 256 only for member households than non-member households. Like wise the average household income of member households are slightly higher than non-member households in all regions (Rs. 323, Rs. 58 and Rs. 328 in central, eastern and western regions respectively). Further the total household income of both member and non-members is higher in eastern region followed by central and western regions.

To study the impact of dairy development through OF on poverty, monthly per capita income of Rs. 168.84 is taken as poverty line as per Planning Commission definition. The incidence of poverty in the study area is as follows. In central region 31 and 58 per cent, in eastern region 20 and 22 per cent and in western region 59 and 69 per cent of population are below poverty line among member and non member households respectively. In the study area 32 per cent of the people in member and 50 per cent in non-member households are in poverty.

The proportion of poor among non-member households is 18 per cent higher than member households in the study area and it varies from region to region. The proportion of poor among non-member households is 27 per cent higher than member households in central region followed by western region (10 per cent) and eastern region (2 per cent). Hence, it can be inferred that impact of OF on poverty is more in central region and less in western region and very negligible in eastern region.

All households below poverty line are not equally poor. The head count ratio does not taken into consideration of the short fall of income below poverty line. Hence, to measure short fall of income Sen poverty measure 'P' is used. It reveals that short fall of income below poverty line is larger to the non-members (0.235) than member households (0.125) in the study area. The 'P' measure further indicates that the short fall of income among poor is more in drought prone western region followed by central region and very much less in agriculturally prosperous eastern region.

Thus though dairy development through Operation Flood Programme has not succeeded to solve the poverty problem completely it succeeded in reduction of 'P', considerably.

Since labour households employed family labour alone in dairy activities and no price is changed directly for family labour. In view of this, actual dairy income is computed to analyse the impact of OF on member household's income. When labour cost accounts 70 per cent of total household's expenditure on dairy, actual dairy income accounts three times higher than net dairy income. As per actual dairy income criterion incidence of poverty has come down to 12.3 per cent in the study area. In central and western regions incidence of poverty has come down to 12.5 per cent and 25 per cent respectively. In eastern region average household income is higher than other two regions and poverty is totally absent. Further, poverty measure 'P' has come down from 0.119 to 0.125 in central region and from 0.236 to 0.0425 in western region. Thus the dairy development through operation flood programme has significant impact on poverty of agricultural labour.

But this successful story of Operation Flood Programme in Andhra Pradesh especially in Rayalaseema has come to an end with the enactment of Industrial policy 1991. In the wake of this policy numerous private dairies rushed into the market and have given a dead blow to the cooperative dairy sector. As a result most of the cooperative dairy unions including the leading Chittoor Dairy Union have become defunct due to their limitations in taking timely decisions on par with private sector.

This changing scenario especially in dairy sector demands further research to analyse the impact of institutional change on milk producers, consumers and on the economy as a whole.

APPENDIX - I

Net Area Irrigated by Sources 1986-87

(in '000 hectares)

Sl.No.	Source	Chittoor	Rayalaseema	A.P.
1.	Canalas	1,120	145	1,780
		(1.1)	(35.1)	(50.1)
2.	Tanks	24,320	45	776
		(24.5)	(11)	(21.8)
3.	Tube wells	1.4	14	193
		(1.4)	(3.3)	(5.5)
4.	Other wells	71.952	197	691
		(72.4)	(47.7)	(19.5)
5.	Other sources	0.640	12	110
		(0.6)	(2.9)	(3.1)
6.	Total	99.307	413	3,550
		(100)	(100)	(100)
7.	Irrigated area more than once	30.504	77	810
		(30.7)	(18.4)	(22.8)
8.	Gross Area irrigated	1,29,811	491	4,360

Source : Bureau of Economics and Statistics, A.P. Statistical Abstract, 1987, p. 131.

APPENDIX - II

Cropping Pattern in Andhra Pradesh 1986-87

(in hectares)

Sl.No.	Crop	Chittoor	Rayalaseema	A.P.
1.	Paddy	57,027	1,96,470	34,59,213
		(13.9)	(8.1)	(29.68)
2.	Bajra	10,524	67,415	3,36,022
		(2.6)	(2.8)	(2.9)
3.	Ragi	18,452	40,078	1,82,635
		(4.5)	(1.6)	(1.6)
4.	Jowar	10,116	3,94,444	16,56,096
		(2.5)	(16.2)	(14.2)
5.	Total food crops	1,80,681	12,67,722	86,08,973
		(44.0)	(52.0)	(73.6)

(Appendix Contd...)

Appendix-II (Contd...)

6.	Groundnut	2,17,823	9,86,951	15,70,561
		(53.1)	(40.5)	(13.4)
7.	Sugarcane	24,133	28,133	1,68,354
		(5.8)	(1.1)	(1.4)
8.	Total non-food crops	2,29,843	11,71,022	30,83,844
		(56.0)	(48.0)	(26.4)
	Total Food and non food crops	**4,10,524**	**24,38,724**	**1,16,92,817**
		(100)	(100)	(100)
9.	Food crops irrigated	95,534	3,40,192	39,06,854
		(52.9)	(26.8)	(45.4)
10.	Non-food crops irrigated	34,277	1,50,320	4,53,216
		(14.9)	(12.8)	(14.7)
11.	Total irrigated land	1,29,811	4,90,512	43,60,070
		(31.6)	(20.1)	(37.3)

Note: Figures in the brackets are percentage to total.

Source: Bureau of Economics and Statistics (A.P) Govt. of A.P. Andhra Pradesh Statistical Abstract, 1987 (Computed).

APPENDIX - III

Bovine and Ovine Stock in Andhra Pradesh 1983-87

Sl.No.	*Category/year*	*Chittoor*	*Rayalaseema*	*A.P.*
1.	**Cross-breed Cattle**			
	1983	71,606	93,049	73,31
	1987	3,90,403	2,08,570	1,64,107
		(125.3)	(124.2)	(129.2)
2.	**Indigenous Cattle**			
	1983	1,30,46,792	23,71,962	8,39,016
	1987	1,19,83,898	21,94,211	6,91,219
		(-8.2)	(-7.5)	(-17.7)
3.	**Total Cattle**			
	1983	1,32,20,110	24,72,175	9,10,622
	1987	1,23,74,301	24,02,811	8,55,324
		(-6.3)	(-2.8)	(-6.0)
4.	**Buffaloes**			
	1983	87,03,873	13,14,908	2,26,950
	1987	87,57,215	13,50,624	2,23,950
		(-0.6)	(+2.7)	(-1.4)

(Appendix Contd...)

Appendix-III (Contd...)

5. **Total Bovine**			
1983	2,19,23,982	37,87,083	11,37,572
1987	2,11,31,516	37,53,435	10,79,045
	(-3.6)	(-0.8)	(-5.1)
6. **Ovine Stock**			
a. Sheep			
1983	75,18,546	22,02,072	5,06,391
1987	68,71,952	19,61,909	5,01,849
	(-8.5)	(-10.9)	(-0.8)
b. Goat			
1983	54,59,186	16,36,007	4,29,435
1987	48,75,823	13,50,762	3,25,589
	(-10.6)	(-17.4)	(-24.1)
7. **Total Ovine**			
1983	9,35,079	38,38,079	1,29,77,732
1987	8,27,438	33,12,671	1,17,47,775
	(11.6)	(13.7)	(-9.5)
8. **Total Bovine + Ovine**			
1983	20,73,398	76,25,162	3,49,01,715
1987	19,06,483	70,66,106	3,28,79,291
	(-8.0)	(-7.3)	(-5.8)

Source: 1. A.P. State Report on Livestock Census 1987, Director of Economics and Statistics, Govt.of A.P. Hyderabad (Computed), pp. 117 to 166 & 315 to 327.

2. A.P. Livestock Census, 1983, p. 158-59, 164 and 165.

APPENDIX - IV
Density of Livestock Population (1987)

(Per sq.km.)

Sl.No.	*Category*	*Andhra Pradesh*	*Rayalaseema*	*Chittoor*
1.	Cross-breed cattle	1.4	3.1	10.8
2.	Indigenous cattle	43.5	32.6	45.6
3.	Total cattle	45.0	35.7	56.5
4.	Buffaloes	31.8	20.1	14.7
5.	Total Bovine	76.8	55.8	71.2

(Appendix Contd...)

Appendix-IV (Contd...)

6.	Ovine stock			
	a. Sheep	24.9	29.2	33.1
	b. Goat	17.7	20.7	21.5
7.	Total Ovine	42.7	49.2	54.6
8.	Total Bovine and Ovine	119.5	105.0	125.8

Source: Andhra Pradesh State Report on Livestock Census 1987, Directorate of Economics and statistics, Govt. of Andhra Pradesh, Hyderabad, pp. 117-166 (Computed).

APPENDIX - V
Veterinary Institutions Services in Andhra Pradesh 1986-87

Sl.No.	*Type of Institution*	*Andhra Pradesh*	*Rayalaseema*	*Chittoor*
1.	Veterinary poly Clinics	17	3	1
		(16,180)	(22,433)	(15,152)
2.	Veterinary Hospitals	262	51	13
		(1,049.9)	(1,319.6)	(1,165.5)
3.	Livestock Supervisory	418	284	77
	Units	(194)	(236.96)	(196.7)
4.	Rural Livestock Units	2,565	515	151
		(107.2)	(130.7)	(100.3)
5.	Total	4,265	835	242
		(64.49)	(78.90)	(62.60)
6.	No.of AI Centres (No.)	2,665	558	201
7.	A.I. Done (in '000)	987.3	282	202.1
8.	Calves born (in '000)	267.8	69.7	50.8

Source: A.P.State Report on Live Stock Census 1987, Directorate of Economic and Statistics, Government of A.P., Hyderabad - 4, P. 397 & 401 (Computed).

Note : Figures in the brackets denote average area (sq.km.) covered by a unit.

APPENDIX - VI

A.K.Sen Poverty Measure (P)

Sen Poverty Measure P = H [I + (1-I) G.

Where,

P = Measure of Poverty

H = Head Count Ratio

I = Income gap Ratio

G = Gini co-efficient,

$$H = \frac{\text{No.of people below poverty line (q)}}{\text{Total Number of population (n)}}$$

$$I = \frac{\text{Weighted Income Gap (g)}}{\text{No.of People below poverty line(q) X Poverty level income (z)}}$$

$$G = \frac{\text{Total weighted income gap}}{\text{Total value of weights}}$$

NOTES AND REFERENCES

1 C.H.Hanumantha Rao, *et al.*, Poverty Eradication in India by the year 2000: Some Macro Economic Implications, Man and Development', December 1985, p. 29.

2 Ibid., p. 29.

3 Poverty Growth and Human Development - A New Integration of Ends and Means, Monthly Commentary on Indian Economic conditions, Blue Supplement, Vol.XXII, No.1, p.1. August, 1981.

4 Ibid., p. 1.

5 Ibid.

6 Sulabha Brahme, "Programmes for the Study of Poverty and Unemployment, ICSSR **Newsletter**, Vol.VIIII (1 & 2), April-September, 1979, pp. 1-18.

7 Keith Griffin., **Land Concentration and Rural Poverty**, The Mac-Millan Press, 1976.

8 E.J.Holswami, **Poverty, International Encyclopedia of the Social Sciences** (New York, 1968), p. 398.

9 B.Seebohn Rowntree, **Poverty, A study of Town Life**, London 1901.

10 Peter Townsend., **Poverty, Inequality and Class Structure**, Cambridge University Press, 1974, pp. 15-41.

11 Rowntree, B.S. **Poverty and Progress**, Longmans, 1941, p. 460.

12 Samuel Mencher., **Poverty**, Penguin Modern Society Readings, (1972), p. 79.

13 World Bank Annual Meeting, Nairobi, Kenya, 24th September, 1973.

14 Ibid.

15 Sastry, S.A.S., Poverty, Concept and Measurement, **Indian Journal of Economics**, October 1980, No. 241.

16 The Poverty line of the seriously poor is equivalent to an income per head of U.S. $ 500 in Western Europe, U.S. $ 180 in Latin America, U.S. $ 115 in Africa and U.S. $ 100 in Asia. Similarly the destitute comprise those with an income equivalent to U.S. $ 250 in West Europe, U.S. $ 90 in Latin America, U.S. $ 59 in Africa and U.S. $ 50 in Asia (1972).

17 I.L.O., Employment, Growth and Basic Needs: A One Word Problem, Praeger Publishers, New York, 1977, p. 20.

18 Santiago Declaration of Third World Economists, 1973.

19 Human Development Report, 1992, UNDP, p. 42.

20 Lief., E. Chestafferson, **Finance and Development**, December, 1978, p. 18.

21 Chenery Hollis *et al.*, **Redistribution with Growth**, London; Oxford University Press, 1974.

22 Rural Poverty Unperceived: Problems and Remedies, **World Bank Staff Working Paper**, No.400, July 1980, p. 6.

23 World Bank Publications, **The Assault on Rural Poverty** (Problems of Rural Development, Education and Health), The Johns Hopkins University Press, London, 1975, pp. 21-24.

24 **World Bank Report Series**, World Bank and The World Poorest, 1980.

25 Ibid.

26 Desai, S.S.M., The Poverty in India, The Magnitude of the Problem, Economic Times, Nov. 1980, p. 5.

27 Govt. of India, Eco**nomic Survey 1993-94**, Ministry of Finance, Economic Division, New Delhi, p. 147; Economic Survey, 2002-2003, p. 213.

28 Dandekar, V.M. and Rath, N.,. Ibid., p. 20.

29 Ibid., p. 23.

30 Mahendra Dev, S., Poverty of Agricultural Households in India: A State level analysis. Indian Journal of Agricultural Economics, January-March, 1988, pp. 14-25.

31 Prabhu Ghate, "Direct Attack on Poverty : Poverty, Programmes and Implications, Concept Publishing Company, New Delhi, 1984.

32 Ibid., p. 3.

33 Rami Reddy, G and Hara Gopal, G., **Public Policy and the Rural Poor in India - A Study of SFDA in Andhra Pradesh**. Centre for Economic and Social Studies, Hyderabad and Concept Publishing Company, New Delhi, 1985.

34 Habsbawm; **Poverty, International Encyclopaedia of Social Sciences**, The Mac Millan Company and The Free Press, London, 1968.

35 Hanumantha Rao, C.H., *et al.*, Poverty Eradication in India by the Year 2000 : Some Macro-Economic Implications, **Man and Development**, December 1985, p. 35.

36 Ibid., p. 35.

37 Govt. of India, Economic Survey 1993-94, Ministry of Finance, p. 148.

38 Government of India., National Commission on Agriculture, Interim Report on Milk Production, 1971, p. 12.

39 Swaminathan, M.S., "Policy Backup Imperative", the Hindu Survey of Indian Agriculture, The Hundu, Madras, 1989.

40 Reserve Bank of India (1989)., A Review of the Agricultural Credit Systems in India : Report of the Agricultural Credit Review Committee (Chairman, A.M. Khusro), Bombay.

41 George P.S. and Nair, K.N. (1990)., Livestock Economy of Kerala, Centre for Development Studies, Trivandrum, Kerala, India, p. 1.

42 Patel, R.K. (1993), Present Status and Promise of Diary in India, **Indian Journal of Agricultural Economics,** January - March, P. 2.

43 Food and Agricultural Organization (1991), FAO Production Year Book,1990, United nations, Rome, Italy,

44 Patel, R.K., Ibid., p. 2.

45 Cows and Buffaloes over three years of breedable age in milk and dry.

46 Patel, R.K., Op.cit., p. 2.

47 Ibid., p. 2-3

48 Ibid., p. 3.

49 Government of India (1976), Report of the National Commission on Agriculture, Part-VII, Animal Husbandry p.2.

50 Government of India (1976), Report of the National commission on Agriculture, Part VII, Animal Husbandry, p. 485.

51 Patel, R.K., Ibid., p. 25.

52 Ibid., p. 3.

53 Ibid.

54 Government of India (1971), Milk production thorough Small and Marginal Farmers and Agricultural labourers: Interim Report of National Commission on Agriculture, National Dairy, Ministry of Agriculture and Irrigation, New Delhi.

55 Khan, R.S., "A Historical Perspective of Dairy Development in India", Indian Dairyman, Vol.41, No.10, Oct. 1989, p. 539.

56 Rao, V.K.R.V., "Some Random Thoughts on Indian Rural and Agricultural Developments:, Guest lecture series No.1, Institute of Rural Management, Anand, Gujarat, 1985.

57 Patel, R.K., Ibid., p. 5.

58 Mittal, J.P. and Shiv Prasad, (1990), Place of Dairy Farming in Arid Agriculture, Indian Dairyman, Vol. 42, No. 1, pp. 17-18.

59 Patel, R.K. (1991), "Role of Livestock Production in Rainfed Agriculture - A Comparative Study, in Proceedings of the International Conference on Technologies for Minimising Risk in Rainfed Agriculture, **Indian Society of Extension Education,** New Delhi, pp. 394-411.

60 Government of India., Report of the National Commission on Agriculture, Part II, Animal Husbandry, 1976, p. 13.

61 Govt. of India, Ibid., p .13.

62 Government of India, Ibid., p. 19.

63 Government of India, Ibid., p. 39.

64 George, P.S. and Nair K.N., Livestock Economy of Kerala, Centre for Development Studies, Trivandrum, Kerala, p. 6.

65 Kurup, M.P.G., Specialised Dairy Farming for Quality Production of Milk, Paper presented at Dairy Industry Conference, New Delhi, 1991.

66 Famine Enquiry commission (1945), Final Report of the Famine enquiry Commission, Govt. Press, Manager Publications, Delhi.

67 Government of India, Op.cit., p. 124.

68 Government of India, (1976), Ibid., p. 126.

69 UN/FAOWFP; Terminal Evaluation Report on Evaluation of Operation Flood and Rural Poor, Project India 618-Milk Marketing and Dairy Development (OF-I), Rome, Sept. 1981. p. 4.

70 National Dairy Development Board (1979), Replication of Anand Pattern Milk producer Cooperative, Anand.

71 Ibid.

72 Halse,M. (1977), India., Operation flood: A study., FAO Report, W/K/9/4, Rome.

73 National Dairy Development Board, Operation Flood-II, A proposal by the National Dairy Development Board, Revised Edition, Anand, 1978.

74 Martin Doornbs *et al.*, Dairy Aid and Development: India's Operation Flood, Sage Publications, New Delhi, (1990), p. 29.

75 UN/FAOWFP 1981, Technical Evaluation Report on Project India 618-Milk Marketing and Dairy Development, (OF-I) Rome, September 1981, p. 17.

76 Martin Doornbs *et al.*, (1990), Dairy aid and Development: India's Operation Flood; Sage Publications, New Delhi, pp. 84-85.

77 National Dairy Development Board, Operation Flood II: A Proposal by the NDDB Revised Edition, Anand 1978, pp. 2-3.

78 Ibid.

79 Martin Doornbos *et al.*,Dairy Aid and Development: India's Operation Flood, Indo-Duch Studies on Development alternatives - 3, Sage publications, New Delhi, 1990. pp. 26-27.

80 Shanti-george, "Operation Flood and Rural India, vested and Divested Interests", Economic and political weekly, December 7, 1985, p. 2168.

81 Shah, V.P., Role of Milk Cooperatives in Articulating Rural Urban Interactions: Experiences in Gujarat, Gujarat University, 1981, p. 56-57.

82 Van Dorstan, F., Milk Marketing and Rural Development: A comparison of the Impact of the Delhi Milk Schemes and the Mehsana

District Cooperatives Milk producers Union, Working paper - Series on Dairy Aid Development, No.22, The Hugue, Institute of Social Studies, July, 1986.

83 Klaus Nyholm *et al.*,'Socio-Economic aspects of Dairy Development - Report from the Bangalore Milk Shed Area' Economic and Political Weekly, December 1974, pp. 127-36.

84 Bowonder, B., Das Gupta, B., Sanjeev Gaupta and Prasad S.S.R., Dairy Development has helped the poor "The Hindu, May 20, 1986.

85 Renede G.G. *et al.*, Performance of Integrated Milk Cooperatives (A study of selected cooperative Dairies in Gujarat and Maharastra) C.M.A. Monograph Series No.III, Indian Institute of Management, Ahmadabad, 1984, p. 174.

86 Binadair, R.D., Changing Village Through Dairy Development - A case study, Changing Village, July-August, 1985, pp.246-247.

87 Sudhakar Reddy, S., Andhra Pradesh Economy in Transition, Centre for Economic and Social studies, Hyderabad pp.507-510 (computed).

88 Hand book of Statistics, 1989-90 Chittoor District, Chittoor, p.62.

89 A.P.State Report on Livestock Census, 1987, Op.cit., pp. 889.

90 Hand Book of Statistics 1991-92, Chittoor district, p. 1.

91 Petel, R.K. (1993), Op.cit., p. 9.

92 Report of the Technology Mission for Dairy Development, Chittoor Dairy cooperative Milk Federation Ltd., Chittoor, p. 28, (1990).

93 NDDB (1990), Appraisal Report on Project proposal of Chittoor District Cooperative Milk Producers Union Limited, Anand, March, p. 1.

94 Kurien, V., The larger dimensions of Dairy Development ? Lecture delivered during sixth Lal Bahadur Sastri Memorial Lecture series at Indian Agricultural Research Institute (Mimeograph), p. 3.

95 Iya, K.K. (1973): Fifty Years of Dairy Development in India-Tasks Ahead, Indian Dairyman, No. 12, December, p. 520.

96 The World Bank, World Development Report, 1984, Oxford, pp. 155-183.

97 Sen, Amartya, "Poverty and Feminine An Essay on Entitlement and Deprivation", Oxford Publishers, Oxford, 1980, pp. 373-387.

Doornbos, M. and M. Mitra, Politics of International Dairy A International Interests and the White Revolution, 1985.

Doornbos, M. and K.N. Nair (Eds.), Resources Institutions and Strategie Operation Flood and Indian Dairying, New Delhi, Sage Publication, 1990.

Dwivedi, D.N. , Economic Concentration and Poverty in India, Dutt Book Centre, Delhi, 1974.

Elliot Charless, Pattern of Poverty in the Third World, A Study of Social and Economic Stratification, Prageur, New York, 1973.

Frank Charles, R., Webb Richard , (eds.), Income Distribution and Growth in the Less Developed Countries, Washington, D.C., Brookings Institution Retaincips, 1977.

Frank Charless, and Webb Richard C., An overall View of Income Distribution and the Growth in the Less Developed Countries, Policy Alternatives and Design, in Frank and Webb, 1977.

Fromser Thomas, M., Culture and Change in India, University of Manchester Press, 1968.

Galbrieth John, K., The Nature of Mass Poverty, Harward University Press, Cambridge, 1979.

Ganguli, B.N. and Gupta, D.B., Levels of Living in India, Chand and Company, New Delhi, 1976.

George Shanti , Operation Flood: An Appraisal of Current Indian Dairy Policy, oxford University Press, New Delhi, 1986.

George G. et al., Farm Level Case Study, Multidesciplinary Field Level Research on Cattle Holdings in six villages of Kerala, Department of Geography, University of Turichy, Irchel, Turich, Switzerland, 1988.

George, S,, Cooperatives of Indian Dairy Policy, More than Anand pattern, Paper presented at Workshop on Cooperatives and Rural Development in India, Delhi University, March, 1983.

——Operation Flood an appraisal of Current Indian Dairy Policy, Oxford University Press, Delhi, 1983.

George, P.S., et al., Policy Options for Cattle Development in Kerala, Kerala Livestock Development Board, Trivandrum, 1989.

Giffen, K. and Khan.; Poverty and Land Less Labour in Rural Asia, International Labour Organisation, Geneva, 1976.

Giffen, K., International Inequality and National Poverty, The Macmillan Press Ltd., 1978.

Hanumantha Rao, C.H., Technological Change, Distribution of Gains in Indian Agriculture, New Delhi, Institute of Economic Growth, 1975.

Haq. Mahbub., The Poverty, Certain Choices for the Third World, Columbia University Press, New York, 1976.

BIBLIOGRAPHY

Adelman. I., Economic Growth and Social Equity in Developing Countries, Stanford University Press, Stanford Clif, 1973.

Adelman. I., and Morris. C.T., Society, Politics and Economic Development, John Hopkins University Press, Baltimore, 1967.

Agarwal. V.K., Economics of Milk Industry in India: Need for Modernisation, New Delhi, Common Wealth Publishers, 1990.

Ahluwalia. M.S., Rural Poverty in India, International Bank for Reconstruction and Development Staff Working Paper, Washington, May, 1979.

Ahluwalia, M.S., Growth and Development in Developing Countries, International Bank for Reconstruction and Development, Staff Working Paper, 1979.

Bardhan, P.K., Poverty of Agricultural Labourers and Trickle down in Rural India, Essays in Development Economics, Oxford University Press, New Delhi, 1984.

Bardhan, P.K., Land, Labour and Rural Poverty, Essays in Development Economics, Oxford Press, New Delhi, 1984.

Baniskar, S.S., EEC Dairy Food Aid to India ISS/IAPAD Working Paper Series, on Dairy Aid and Development, 1986.

Baniskar, S.S, and P. Terhal., International Constraints and External Dependence EEC and Operation Flood (in M. Doornbos and K.N- Nair (Eds.) Operation Flood and Indian Dairying, New Delhi, 1990).

Bhalla, G.S. and G.K. Chandra, Green; Revolution and the Small Peasant, Concept Publishing Company, New Delhi, 1983.

Bhanja, S.K. and S. Venkatadri, Milch Cattle in Rural Development Programme, National Institute of Rural Development, Hyderabad, India, 1988.

Centre for Education and Documentation; Operation Flood : Development or Dependence, Cite Publications, Bombay, 1982.

Chenery Hollis, et al. , Redistribution and Growth in England, Oxford University Press, 1974.

Coombs Phillip (ed.), Meeting the Basic needs of the Rural Poor' Integrated Community based Approaches, New York, Pergamon, 1980.

Dandekar, V.M. and Rath, N., Poverty in India, Indian School of Political Economy, Poone, 1971.

Dantwala, M.L., Poverty in India, Now and Then (1870-1970) Macmillan Company, New Delhi, 1973.

Devitt Paul. , Notes on Poverty Oriented Rural Development in Extension Planning and the Poor, London, Overseas Development Institute, 1977.

I.B.R.D., Small Farmers and the Land less in the South Asia' Staff Working Paper, No.320, Feb. 1979.

I.L.O., Employment Growth and Basic Needs - A One World Problem, Geneva, 1976.

I.L.O., Poverty and Landless in Rural Asia, Geneva, 1977.

I.L.O., Labour Absorption in Indian Agriculture, Some Exploratory Investigation, I.L,0., Bangkok, 1978.

I.L.O., Profiles of Rural Poverty, Geneva, 1980.

Jain, J.L.A., Prasad and G.N. Gupta., Organised Milk Marketing in India, Socio-Economic Impact (A Study of the Delhi Milk Scheme in N.W. Rajastan), Kumarappa Institute of Gram Swaraj, Jaipur, 1982.

Jha, Shailendra, Agricultural Labour : Present Position, Problems and Legislations and Govt., Measures for Upliftment, Deep and Deep Publications, New Delhi, 1990.

Jorgenson, D.W., Surplus, Agricultural Labour and the Development of Dual Economy, Oxford Economic Papers, Vol.9, 1967.

Jorgenson, D.W., The Role of Agriculture in Economic Development, Classical Versus, Neo-classical Model of Growth, Chicago, 1969.

Keith Giffen., Land Concentration and Rural Poverty, The Macmillan Press, 1976.

Khurody, D-N., Dairying in India, A Review; Asian Publishing House, Bombay, 1974.

Kulandaiswamy, V., Cooperative Dairying in India, Rainbow Publications, Coimbatore, India.

Kurup, M.P,G., Specialised Dairy Farming for Quality of Milk Production, Paper presented at Dairy Industry Conference, New Delhi, 1991.

Kurien, C.T., Poverty, Planning and Social Transformation, Allied Publishers, New Delhi, 1978.

Leaver, J.D., Milk Production Sciences and Practices, Longman Group Ltd., London, 1983.

Martin Doornbos., et al., Dairy Aid and Development, Indias Operation Flood, Indo-Duch Studies on Development Alternatives, 3, Sage Publications, New Delhi, 1990.

Masacrenhar, R.C., A Strategy for Rural Development and Dairy Cooperatives in India, Sage Publications, New Delhi, 1988.

Mehra Shakuntala., Some Aspects of Labour use in Indian Agriculture, occasional Paper, Department of. Agricultural Economics, Cornell University.

Mergas, G. and R. Slade., Dairy Development and Milk Co-operatives, World Bank Discussion Papers, Washington, 1987.

Minnas, B.S., Planning and the poor, S. Chand and Company, New Delhi, 1976.

Mishra, S.N., Livestock Planning in India, Vikas Publishing House, New Delhi, 1978.

Mohan., N. Impact of Dairy Cooperatives on Poverty groups in the Operation Flood Areas, National Institute of Rural Development, Hyderabad, India.

Moulik Tushar, Kanti., Strategies of Implementation of Rural Development Programmes in India, Indian Institute of Management Working Paper, Ahmedabad.

Myrdal Gunnar., Asian Drama: An enquiry into the Poverty of Nations, 20th Century Fund, Penguin Books, New York, 1968.

Naidu, M.D. Narayana, Poverty and Development in Indian Villages, Tirupati, S.V.University, 1990.

Olson, T.M., Elements of Dairying, VIIth edition, Mac Miilan Company, New York, 1960.

Peter Townsend., Poverty, Inequality and Class Structure, Cambridge University Press, 1974.

Prabhu Ghate., Direct attack on Poverty, Poverty Programmes and Implications, Concept Publishing Company, New Delhi, 1984.

Rajaraman Indira., Constructing the Poverty Line, Rural Punjab Discussion Paper No.43, Research Programme in Economic Development Woodrow Wilson & Annual Number 277, 1973.

Rami Reddy, G. and Haragopal, G., Public Policy and the Rural Poor in India, A Study of SFDA in Andhra Pradesh, (Centre for Economic and Social Studies, Hyderabad), Concept Publishing Company, New Delhi, 1985.

Rao, V.K.R.V., Some Random thoughts on Indian Rural Agricultural Developments, Guest Lecture, Series No. Ill, Indian Institute of Management, Ahmadabad, 1984.

Rao, V.K.R.V., Random thoughts on Indian Rural and Agricultural Developments, Guest Lecture, Series No.I, Institute of Rural Management, Anand Gujarat, 1985.

Ranedy, G.G., et al., Performance of Integrated Milk Cooperatives (A Study of Selected Cooperatives Dairies in Gujarat and Maharastra) (M.A. Monograph Series No.Ill, Indian Institute of Management, Ahmedabad, 1984.

Sambrani, S., et al., A comparative Cost to Milk Production, Eastern Economist, May, 1981.

Shangani, P., Surplus Manpower in Agriculture and Economic Development, Asia Publishing House, Bombay, 1969.

Singh, V.P., Role of Milk Cooperatives in Articulating Rural and Urban, Interactions, Experience in Gujarat, Gujarat University, 1981.

Srivastava, R.K., Impact of Cattle Development Programmes 'on Rural Economy of the Kaira District, KDCMPU Ltd., 1970.

Srivastava, T.N. and Bardhan, P.K. (ed .) , Poverty and Income Distribution in India, Statistical Publishing Society, Calcutta, 1974.

Seebohm Rowntree., Poverty, A Study of Town Life, London, 1901.

Thakur, D.S., Benefits of Milk Cooperatives to Small Farmers Marginal Farmers and the Land Less in Gujarat, NDDB, 1977.

Todaro Michael, P. Economics for Developing World, Longman Group Limited, London, 1977.

Townsend Peter (ed.), The Concepts of Poverty, Heinemann, London, 1970.

Townsend, P., Poverty as Relative Deprivation, Resources and Style of Living (ed.) Wedderbun, 1974.

Uppal, J.S., Disguised Unemployment in an Underdeveloped Economy, Its Nature and Measurement, Asian Publishing House, New Delhi, 1973.

Vaidyanadhan, A., Labour Use in Indian Agriculture, an analysis based on Farm Management Data in ILO, 1978.

Vaidyanadhan, A., Role of Bovines in Indian Agriculture, A study of Size, Composition and Productivity, Centre for Development Studies, Trivandrum (Kerala), 1982.

Vakil, C.N., Poverty Planning and Inflation, Allied Publishers Private Limited, 1978.

Van, F., Dorstan., Milk Marketing and Rural Development : A Comparison of the Impact of the Delhi Milk Schemes and the Mehsana District Cooperative Milk Producers Union, Working Paper, Series on Dairy Aid and Development No. 22, The Hague Institute of Social Studies, July 1986.

Vasaria Praveen., Poverty and Living Standards in Asia, An overview of the Main Results, and Lesson of Selected Household Surveys, Living Standards Measurement Study, World Bank, October,1980.

World Bank., Rural Poverty Unperceived Problems and Remedies, World Bank Staff Working Paper, No.400, July 1980.

World Bank Publications, The Assault on Rural Poverty (Problems of Rural Development Education and Health), John Hopkins, University Press, London, 1975.

JOURNALS

Abraham Amrita., Maharastra Employment Scheme, Economic and Political Weekly, August, 1980.

Acharya, S.S., Green Revolution and Farm Employment, Indian Journal of Agricultural Economics, 1973.

Acharya Apiad., The Economics of Milk Production in different animals, Indian Journal of Agricultural Economics, 1980.

Adiseshaiah Malcolm, S., Three causes of our growing Poverty, Hindustan Times, 1976.

Ahluwalia, M.S., Rural Poverty and Agricultural Performance in India, The Journal of Development, April, 1973.

Ahluwalia Montek. S., Policies for Poverty Alleviation, Asian Development Review, 1990.

Bachman M.R., Milk Production and Transformation in Less Developed Countries, International Journal of Development of Technology, 1985.

Balakrishna, S., Incidence of Rural Poverty in Recent Years, Behavioural Science and Rural Development, January, 1980.

Bal, H.S., Economics of Milch Animals and Farm Size Analysis, Indian Journal of Agricultural Economics, 1980.

Baldev, Singh., Economics of Milk Production and Bovine Livestock Composition in Grouping Economy, Indian Economic Journal, 1979.

Bardhan Kalpana., Rural Employment wages and Labour Markets in India, A Survey of Research, Economic and Political Weekly, 1977.

Bardhan, P.K., Operation Flood its Evolution, the Strategy followed and Progress achieved, Indian Dairyman, 1981.

Bardhan, P.K., Factors Affecting Wage rates for Agricultural Labour, Economic and Political Weekly, 1973.

Bardhan, P.K., On the Incidence of Rural Poverty in India in the Sixties, Economic and Political Weekly, 1973.

Bardhan, P.K., On the Minimum Level of Living and the Rural Poor, Indian Economic Review, April, 1971.

Bardhan, P.K., The Green Revolution and Agricultural Labourers, Economic and Political Weekly, 1970.

Baviskar, B.S. , Some Aspects of Dairy Development in Gujarat and Karnataka, World Bank Review, 1983.

Baviskar, B.S., Milk Cooperatives and Rural Development in Gujarat: A Case Study, Paper presented at Symposium on Cooperatives and Rural Development, Valmorin (Canada),1983.

Bedi, M.S., Operation Flood, its evolution, the strategy followed and progress achieved, Indian Dairyman, 1981.

Bhatty, F.Z., Inequality and Poverty in Rural India, in Sankya Series, C, Vol.36, 1974.

Bhanja, S.K. and Venkatadri, S., Cattle for Indian Rural Poor, Rural Development in Practice, National Institute for Rural Development, 1990.

Biradar, R.D., Rural development through dairy development - A Case Study, Kurukshetra, Vol. 30, 1982.

Bewonder B., et al., Dairy Development has helped the poor, The Hindu, May 20, 1986.

Binadair, R.D., Changing Village through Dairy Development: A Case Study, Changing Villages, July, 1985.

Breman Jan., Mobilization of Land less Labourers, Halpatis of South Gujarat, Economic and Political Weekly, March 23, 1974.

Chauhan, J.S, Dairy development goes to a pace, Economic Times, Supplementary, July, 1980.

Chakravarthy, T.K., and C.0. Reddy, Dairy Development Programme Process and Impact, A Study at Village Level, Journal of Rural Development, 1982.

Chambers Robert R. Longhurst, D. Bradly and R.Teachem, Seasonal dimensions to Rural Poverty, Analysis and Practical Implications Discussion, Paper-42, Institute of Development Studies, 1979.

Cherunilam, Franasis., Rural Poverty Causes and Cures, Yojana, 1980.

Chowdhary, R.K., Structural Malady Behind in Equality of Income Distribution in India, Indian Economic Journal, Dec., 1978.

Clark Stephen, et al., On Indices for the Measurement of Poverty, Indian Economic Journal, 1981.

Das Bhagavan and Kuber Raw., Impact of Dairy Cooperation on Marketing Surplus of Milk in the Firms in the Milk shed area of Ralkuar Milk Plant, National Indian Cooperatives Review, 1981.

Desai, S.S.M., Poverty in India, The Magnitude of the Problem, Economic Times, November, 1980.

Divitia, V.V., Inequality in assets distribution of rural households, Reserve Bank of India Staff Papers, Vol. 1(1), June 1976.

Dupan, T.C., and Singh, C.B., Progress and Prospects of Dairy Development through Cooperatives in Haryana State, Indian Cooperative Review, April, 1982.

Gadgil, D.R., Pre-Conditions of Economic Development, Indian Journal of Economics, February, 1952.

Ganguii, B.K-, Changing face of Dairying in India, A Case Study in Ghanshayampur in Murshidabad, West Bengal, Journal of Rural Development, 1985.

George, P.S., and U.K. Srivastava, Institutional Finance for Dairy Development, Indian Economic Journal, 1975.

Grewal, S.S. and P.S. Rangi., Economics and Employment of Dairying in Punjab, Indian Journal of Agricultural Economics, October, December, 1980.

Hanumantha Rao., C.H., Green Revolution and Labour share in output, Agricultural Situation in India, August, 1971.

——Farm Machanisation in Labour Abundant Economy, Economic and Political Weekly, February, 1972.

——Poverty and Development Characteristics of Less Developed Regions in India, Economic and Political Weekly, Special No. August, 1979.

——et al., Poverty Erradication in India by the year 2000, Some Macro Economic Implications, Man and Development, December, 1985.

Hanumantha Rao, C.H., Poverty Development Characteristics of Less Developed Regions in India, Economic and Political Weekly, 1979.

Hanumantha Rao, K., and Sastry, K.V.S., Levels of Living and Poverty among Social Groups in A-P., A Cross Section Analysis, Journal of Rural, Development, January, 1990.

Huria, V.K. and K.T. Acharya., Dairy Development in India, Some Critical Issues, Economic and Political Weekly, 1980.

Indian Institute of Public Opinion, The Measurement of Deprevation by degrees of Destination in Indian State 1973-74, Quarterly Economic Report, Vol. XXIV, 1978.

Jain, J.L., et al., Organised Milk Marketing in India, Socio-Economic Impact, Kumarappa Institute of Gram Swaraj, Jaipur, 1982.

Jain, M.M*, Dairy Development through Cooperatives : A Study of Rajastan, Indian Dairy Man, 1980.

Jain, L.R., and *et al.*, Dimensions of Rural Poverty, An Inter Regional Profile, Economic and Political Weekly, November, 1988.

.Jeemol, Unni., Agricultural Labourers in Rural Labour House Holds, Changes in Employment Wages and Income, Economic and Political Weekly, June 25, 1988.

Jodha, M.S., Special Programmes for the Rural Poor, The Constraining Framework, Economic and Political Weekly, March 31, 1973.

Joshi, T., Ravi and Prabhakar, B., Impact of Dairy Scheme Bovine Population in Haryana, A District wise Analysis, Agricultural Situation in India, January, 1989.

Jose, A.V., Trends in Rural Wage rates of Agricultural Labourers, Economic and Political Weekly, 1974.

Kalyankar, S.P., Economics of Milch Production in different Cows and Buffaloes, Indian Journal of Agriculture Economics, 1980.

Kaur, M., and Sharma, M.L., Role of Farm Women in Animal Husbandary, Study of Haryana, Indian Dairy Man, 1985.

Khanna, R.S., A Historical Prospects of Dairy Development in India, Indian Dairy Man, Vol. 41, 1989.

Klaus Nyholm, et al., Socio-economic aspects of Dairy Development - Report from the Bangalore Milk Shed Area, Economic and Political Weekly, 1974.

Krishna Raj-, Unemployment in India, Indian Journal of Agricultural Economics, Vol.28 , March 1973.

Krishna Raj., Income, Poverty and Unemployment, Economic Times, May 15, 1980.

Kurian, K., Indegeneous Milk Products of India, Present and future market share, Indian Dairyman, 1990.

Lalwani Mahesh., Human Labour absorption in Dairying' Evidence from Karnal Villages, Haryana, Indian Journal of Agricultural Economics, 1990.

Lalwani, Mahesh., Resource use Efficiency, A Study of Dairy Farmers Social Action, July, 1990.

Laldeepak., Agricultural Growth' real wages and Rurai Poor in India, Economic and Political Weekly, 1976.

Lewis, A.L., Economic Development with Unlimited Supplies of Labour, Manchester School of Economics and Social Studies, 22, 1954.

Madalia, U.K. and Charaw, U-K., Economics of Main Finance of Cows and Buffaloes and their Milk Production, Indian Journal of Agricultural Economics, September, 1975.

Mahendra Dev , S. , Poverty of Agricultural Labour Households in India, A State Level Analysis, Indian Journal of Agricultural Economics, January, 1988.

Madiman, S.G., and N.K. Desai, Cost of Producing Milk in Anand Area, Indian Journal of Agricultural Economics, 1951.

Mehra Shakuntala., Surplus Labour in Indian Agriculture, Indian Economic Review, Vol.1, April, 1966.

Mittal, J.P.M., Siva Prasad, Place of Dairy Farming in Arid Agriculture, Indian Dairyman, vol. 42, January, 1990.

Moor, M.P. , Some Micro Economic Aspects of the Livestock Economy, Indian Journal of Agricultural Economics, Vol.33, 1978.

Moulik, Tushar Kanti, Strategies of Implementation of Rural Developmental Programmes in India, Indian Institute of Management, Working Paper 269, Ahmedabad, 1979.

NABARD., Financing Programmes for Poverty Alleviation Problems and Issues, Journal of Rural Development, January 1990.

Nair, K.N., Operation Flood Some Constraints and Implications, Economic and Political Weekly, 1990.

Nair, K.N., White Revolution in India, Facts and Issues, Economic and Political Weekly, 1985.

Nair, K.N., Breeding and Feeding of Milk Production in Operation Flood II, Economic and Political Weekly, Vol.XVI, 1981.

Nair, K.N., Milk Production in Kerala, Trends - Prospects, Economic and Political Weekly, Vol.24, 1979.

Nair, K.N., and M.G. Jackson, Alternative to Operation Flood-II, and A Strategy, Economic and Political Weekly, December 26, 1981.

Nata Raju, M.S., and Channegowala, M.B., Differential adoption of Improved Dairy Practices by Small Farmers, Marginal and Agricultural Labourers, Indian Journal of External Education, 1987.

Paglin, M., Surplus Agricultural Labour and Development, Facts and Figures, The American Economic Review, Vol.55, 1965.

Pant, K.C., Estimates of Milk Production in India, Cooperative Dairying, July, 1981.

Panikar, P.G.K., Employment, Income and Food Intake among elected agricultural labour households, Economics and Political Weekly, 1978.

Parthasaradhy, G. and K. Adiseshu, Real Wages of Agricultural Labourers in Andhra Pradesh, Two Decades of Stagnation, Economic and Political Weekly, 1982.

Parthasaradhy, G. and G.D. Rama Rao, Minimum Wages Legislation for Agricultural Labour: A Review of Agriculture, Economic and.Political Weekly, September, 1975.

Pat el, R.K., Peasant Status and Provision of Dairy in India, Indian Journal of Agricultural Economics, March, 1993.

Patel, R.K., Role of Livestock Production in Rainfed Agriculture : A Comparative Study in Proceedings of International Conference of Technologies for Minimising Risk in Rainfed Agriculture, Indian Society of Extension Education, New Delhi, 1991.

Raj Krishna, Unemployment in India, Economic and Political Weekly, March, 1973.

Rajapurohit, A.R., Cross Breeding of Indian Cattle, An Evolution, Economic and Political Weekly, 1979.

Raj, K.N-, Investment in Livestock in Agrarian Economy, Indian Economic Review, Vol.IV, 1969.

Raghavendra, C.V. and Narayana, E.A., Implementation of Dairy Development Schemes at the Gross Roots Level, The Case of Sangam Dairy, Indian Journal of Public Administration, December, 1984.

Rana, R.P.S., Dairies to Irradicate Poverty, Khadigramodayog, August, 1982.

Rajiv Singh and Saine, S., Dairy Enterprises and Small Farmers, Eastern Economist, June, 1979.

Rudra, A., Direct Estimation of Surplus Labour in Agriculture, Economic and Political Weekly, 1973.

Saini, S., et al., A Comparative Cost to Milk Production, Eastern Economist, May, 1981.

Sangani Prapulla, Surplus Man Power in Agricultural Tenancy, Economic and Political Weekly, 1972.

Sastry, S.A.R., A Method of Estimating Surplus Labour in peasant Agriculture in Over Populated Underdeveloped countries, Journal of the Royal Statistical Society, March, 1980.

Sen, A.K., Poverty in equality and Unemployment, Economic and Political Weekly, 1973.

Sastry, S-A.S., Poverty Concept and Measurement, Indian Journal of Economics, 1980.

Shanti George, Deffusing Anand, Implications of Establishing a Dairy Cooperative in a Village in Central Kerala, Economic and Political Weekly, December 22, 1984.

Shanti George, Operation Flood and Rural India, Wested and Divested interests, Economic and Political Weekly, 1985.

Shergill, H.S., Regional Variations in Rural Poverty in India, Pattern and Determinants, Indian Journal of Economics, April, 1981.

Singh, R.B. and et al., A Glance at Operation Flood Phase I, Indian Dairyman, November, 1981.

Singh Katar, The Cooperative as an Organisation for Dairy Development: Lesson of India Experience, IASSI, Quarterly Bulletin, July-October, 1988.

Sinha, J.N., Rural Employment and Planning, Dimensions and Constants, Economic and Political Weekly, Annual Number, February, 1978.

Sinha, J.N., Rural Employment Planning, Dimensions and Constraints, Economic and Political Weekly, February, 1978.

Singh, S., Operation Flood II, Some Constraints and Implications, Economic and Political Weekly, 1979.

Singh, A.S., and Sing., R.V., Impact of Dairy Enterprise on productivity and Employment, Agricultural Situation in India, 1977.

Singh, S. and S. Singh, Commodity Aid : Feed, Export and Operation Flood, Economic and Political Weekly, 1980.

Sukhala, P.V., Assessment of Adequacy of Diets at Different Income Levels, Economic and Political Weekly, August, 1978.

Sulabha, Brahme, Programme for the Study of Poverty and Unemployment, ICSSR News Letter, 1979.

Tewari, R.T-, Inter-regional disparities in levels of Development, Indian Experience, Man and Development, 1983.

Thakur, D.S., A Survey of Literature on Rural Poverty in India, Margin, April, 1985.

Tiruvakkarasu, M. and et al., Impact of Operation Flood on the Income and Employment of Rural Poor, Some micro level evidence, Journal of Rural Development, July 1990

Thorner Daniel, The Agricultural Labour Enquiry, Reflection on concepts and methods, Economic and Political Weekly, June 23, 1956.

Vidya Nathan, A., Some Aspects of Inequalities in Living Standards in Rural Area, Sankya, Voi.36, 1974.

Walle Deminigue Vande, Policies for Reducing Poverty, Finance and Development, September, 1990.

REPORTS

Centre for Monitoring Indian Economy, Basic Statistics Relating to the Indian Economy, Intelligence Service, All India, Bombay, 1989.

Centre for Monitoring Economy, Basic Statistics Relating to the Indian Economy Intelligence Service, All India, Bombay, 1992.

Commission of the European Communities, Report from the Commission to the Council and the European Parliament on the Implementation of India's Operation Flood-11 COM (86), March, 1986.

Commission Report of the Services to the Council and European Parliament on Community support to India's Dairy Industry Development 1365, Brussels, 1987.

Famine Enquiry Commission, Final Report, Government Press, Manager Publications, Delhi, 1945.

Government of India, 7th Five Year Plan, 1985-90, Vol.1, Planning Commission, New Delhi.

Government of India, 7th Five Year Plan, Mid Term Appraisal (1985-90), Planning Commission, New Delhi.

Government of India, The National Sample Survey and Organisation of Sarvekshana, Ministry of Planning, Department of Statistics, New Delhi, 1978.

Government of India, Food and Agricultural Organisation, Production Year Book, 1990.

Government of India, Sixth Five Year Plan, 1980-85, Planning Commission, New Delhi.

Government of India, Milk Production through Small and Marginal Farmers and Agricultural Labourers, Interim Report of National

Commission on Agriculture, Ministry of Agriculture and Irrigation, New Delhi, 1971.

Government of India, Ministry of Agriculture, Report of the Evaluation Committee on Operation Flood II, Jha Committee Report, New Delhi, 1984.

——planning Commission Project Appraisal Division, Appraisal of Operation Flood II, Proposal for Consideration of Public Investment Board, New Delhi, 1978.

——planning Commission, Brief mote on Operation Flood II, New Delhi, 1983.

——Public Investment Board, Memorandum on Operation Flood II, For Consideration of Public Investment Board, Govt. of India, 1985.

Government of India, Interium Report on Milk Production, 1971.

Government of India, Ministy of Labour, Agricultural Labourer in India, Report of IInd Labour Enquiry Committee, New Delhi, 1959.

National Commission on Agriculture (Govt. of India), Interium Report of the National Commission on Agriculture on Milk production through small and marginal farmers and Agricultural labourer, New Delhi, 1971.

——Report of the National Commission on Agriculture, Part-VII, Animal Husbandary, New Delhi, 1976.

——Operation Flood II, A proposal by the National Dairy Development Board, Revised Edition, Anand, 1978.

——Operation Flood-II Techno Economic Feasibility, January (1978 b).

——Replication of Anand Pattern Milk Producers Cooperatives, 1979.

——Operation Flood II Status Report, February, 1981.

——Operation Flood I and II, Retrospects and Prospects, Delhi, 1982 b.

——Operation Flood Phase III, A Proposal by the National Dairy Development Board Anand, 1985.

National Commission on Agriculture Part-Ill, Animal Husbandary, Ministry of Agriculture and Irrigation, Govt. of India, 1976.

National Dairy Development Board: Village Enumeration, A Causes of six million households in 20,386 Dairy Cooperative Villages spread over IO milk sheds, 1984.

N.D.D.B. Operation Flood II , A Proposal Revised Edition, Anand, 1978.

Reserve Bank of India, A Review of the Agricultural Credit Systems in India, Report of the Agricultural Credit Review Committee, 1989.

Rural Labour Inquiry, Labour Bureau, Ministry of Labour, Government of India, Chandigarh, 1980.

UN,FAO WFP., Terminal Evaluation Report on Evaluation of Operation Flood and Rural Poor Project of India, 618 Milk Marketing and Dairy Development (OF-I), Rome, September, 1981.

UN,FAO WFP., Interium Evaluation of WFP assisted Project of India, 618 Milk Marketing and Dairy Development, 1972.

UN,FAO WFP., Terminal Evaluation Report on Project, India 618, Milk Marketing and Dairy Development, 1981.

World Bank Reprint Series, World Bank and World Poorest, 1980.

World Development Report, Oxford University Press, London, 1990.

World Bank, Staff Appraisal Report on National Dairy Project Indian Report, No.1964, in World Bank, Washington, 1978.